50% OFF!

FTCE General Knowledge Online Test Prep Course

We consider it an honor and a privilege that you chose our FTCE General Knowledge Study Guide. As a way of showing our appreciation and to help us better serve you, we have partnered with Mometrix Test Preparation to offer you 50% off their online FTCE General Knowledge Prep Course.

Mometrix has structured their online course to perfectly complement your printed study guide. Many FTCE General Knowledge courses are needlessly expensive and don't deliver enough value. With their course, you get access to the best FTCE General Knowledge prep material, and you only pay half price.

WHAT'S IN THE FTCE GENERAL KNOWLEDGE TEST PREP COURSE?

- ✓ **FTCE General Knowledge Study Guide**: Get access to content that complements your study guide.

- ✓ **Progress Tracker**: Their customized course allows you to check off content you have studied or feel confident with.

- ✓ **550+ Practice Questions**: With 550+ practice questions and lesson reviews, you can test yourself again and again to build confidence.

- ✓ **FTCE General Knowledge Flashcards**: Their course includes a flashcard mode consisting of over 620 content cards to help you study.

TO RECEIVE THIS DISCOUNT, VISIT THE WEBSITE AT

link.mometrix.com/ftcegk

USE THE DISCOUNT CODE:
STARTSTUDYING

IF YOU HAVE ANY QUESTIONS OR CONCERNS, PLEASE CONTACT MOMETRIX AT SUPPORT@MOMETRIX.COM

Mometrix ONLINE COURSES

FREE DVD   FREE   FREE DVD

Essential Test Tips DVD from Trivium Test Prep

Dear Customer,

Thank you for purchasing from Cirrus Test Prep! Whether you're looking to join the military, get into college, or advance your career, we're honored to be a part of your journey.

To show our appreciation (and to help you relieve a little of that test-prep stress), we're offering a **FREE *FTCE Essential Test Tips DVD**** by Cirrus Test Prep. Our DVD includes 35 test preparation strategies that will help keep you calm and collected before and during your big exam. All we ask is that you email us your feedback and describe your experience with our product. Amazing, awful, or just so-so: we want to hear what you have to say!

To receive your **FREE *FTCE Essential Test Tips DVD***, please email us at 5star@cirrustestprep.com. Include "Free 5 Star" in the subject line and the following information in your email:

1. The title of the product you purchased.
2. Your rating from 1 – 5 (with 5 being the best).
3. Your feedback about the product, including how our materials helped you meet your goals and ways in which we can improve our products.
4. Your full name and shipping address so we can send your **FREE *FTCE Essential Test Tips DVD*.**

If you have any questions or concerns please feel free to contact us directly at 5star@cirrustestprep.com.

Thank you, and good luck with your studies!

* Please note that the free DVD is <u>not included</u> with this book. To receive the free DVD, please follow the instructions above.

FTCE General Knowledge Test Prep 2025-2026:

470+ Practice Questions and Florida Teacher Certification Exam Study Guide

8th Edition

Eric Canizales

Copyright © 2025 by Cirrus Test Prep

ISBN-13: 9781637988886

ALL RIGHTS RESERVED. By purchase of this book, you have been licensed one copy for personal use only. No part of this work may be reproduced, redistributed, or used in any form or by any means without prior written permission of the publisher and copyright owner. Cirrus Test Prep; Trivium Test Prep; Accepted, Inc.; and Ascencia Test Prep are all imprints of Trivium Test Prep, LLC.

Pearson Education, Inc. was not involved in the creation or production of this product, is not in any way affiliated with Cirrus Test Prep, and does not sponsor or endorse this product. All test names (and their acronyms) are trademarks of their respective owners. This study guide is for general information only and does not claim endorsement by any third party.

Image(s) used under license from Shutterstock.com

Table of Contents

Online Resources i
Introduction iii

ONE: Writing the Essay 1
    Types of Essays 1
    Writing a Thesis Statement 5
    Structuring the Essay 6
    Supporting Evidence 8
    Writing Well 9
    Example Essays 12

TWO: English Language Skills 15
    Parts of Speech 15
    Constructing Sentences 22
    Avoiding Common Usage Errors 30
    Answer Key 39

THREE: Reading Skills 41
    Introduction 41
    The Main Idea 42
    Supporting Details 45
    Facts and Opinions 48
    Making Inferences 49
    Understanding the Author 50
    Meaning of Words and Phrases 57
    Comparing Passages 66
    Answer Key 68

FOUR: Mathematics 73
Number Sense, Concepts, and Operations 73
Geometry and Measurement 84
Algebraic Thinking and the Coordinate Plane 91
Probability, Statistics, and Data Interpretation 99
Answer Key 107

FIVE: Practice Test 113
The Essay 113
Writing 114
Reading 125
Mathematics 140
Answer Key 149

Online Resources

Cirrus Test Prep includes online resources with the purchase of this study guide to help you fully prepare for your FTCE General Knowledge exam.

Practice Test
In addition to the practice test included in this book, we also offer an online exam. Since many exams today are computer based, practicing your test-taking skills on the computer is a great way to prepare.

Review Questions
Need more practice? Our review questions use a variety of formats to help you memorize key terms and concepts.

Flash Cards
Cirrus Test Prep's flash cards allow you to review important terms easily on your computer or smartphone.

Cheat Sheets
Review the core skills you need to master the exam with easy-to-read Cheat Sheets.

From Stress to Success
Watch From Stress to Success, a brief but insightful YouTube video that offers the tips, tricks, and secrets experts use to score higher on the exam.

Reviews
Leave a review, send us helpful feedback, or sign up for Cirrus promotions—including free books!

Access these resources at:
www.cirrustestprep.com/ftce-general-knowledge-online-resources

Introduction

Congratulations on choosing to take the Florida Teacher Certification Examinations: General Knowledge Test (GK) (082)! By purchasing this book, you've taken the first step toward becoming a teacher, an enriching and satisfying career.

This guide will provide you with a detailed overview of the FTCE General Knowledge Test (GK) (082), so you know exactly what to expect on test day. It will prepare you for all four of the GK subtests: Essay (825), English Language Skills (ELS) (826), Reading (827), and Mathematics (828). We'll take you through all the concepts covered on these tests and give you the opportunity to test your knowledge with practice questions. Even if it's been a while since you last took a major test, don't worry; we'll make sure you're more than ready!

What is the FTCE GK (082)?

The FTCE GK Test is used in the state of Florida to measure teacher candidates' aptitude in mathematics, reading, language skills, and writing. You may take the subtests individually on separate dates, or you may take them all on the same date; either way you must complete all four subtests in order to pass the exam. While you may also be required to take other FTCE tests for specific academic subjects, the core subjects tested on the FTCE GK are essential for anyone entering the teaching profession.

What's on the FTCE GK (082)?

The General Knowledge Test gauges college-level skills in mathematics, reading, language skills, and writing in accordance with the Common Core State Standards. Each test—Mathematics, Reading, English Language Skills, and Writing—is broken down into different categories based on the skills needed to succeed in a teacher preparation program.

The Mathematics (828) subtest focuses on numbers, algebraic thinking, geometry, and statistics and probability. A four-function calculator will appear on-screen when you are permitted to use one. You also will be provided a mathematics reference sheet with important formulas.

On the Reading (827) subtest, you will read and answer questions about fiction and nonfiction passages, which will be of varying length. Some will be paired. They may be taken from any kind of reading material an educated adult is likely to encounter, including novels, newspapers, magazines, articles on current events, and visual representations.

The English Language Skills (ELS) (826) subtest focuses on vocabulary, word choice and language structure. You will answer questions about the language used in specific sentences or short passages.

The Essay (825) subtest measures your ability to analyze purpose, production, and types of text, and your language and compositional skills. You will write one essay.

For all multiple-choice questions, you will select the best answer from either three or four answer options.

What's on the FTCE: General Knowledge Test (082)?

Section	Concepts	Number of Questions	Time
Essay	Purpose, audience, text structure, argument or claim, supporting details, language skills	1 essay	50 minutes
English Language Skills	Language structure, vocabulary application, standard English conventions	40 multiple-choice questions	40 minutes
Reading	Key ideas and details, craft and structure, integration of information and ideas	40 multiple-choice questions	55 minutes
Mathematics	Number sense, concepts, and operations; geometry and measurement; algebraic thinking; probability, statistics, and data interpretation	45 multiple-choice questions	1 hour, 40 minutes
Total		125 questions (and 1 essay)	4 hours and 5 minutes

How is the FTCE GK (082) Scored?

Your scores for the ELS, Reading, and Mathematics subtests become available on your online account within four weeks of the exam, although you will be able to see an unofficial score immediately upon finishing the subtest. You will be notified via email when they are released. It can take up to an additional two weeks to receive your scores from the Essay subtest. Once your scores are posted, they will only remain available for 60 days. Your FTCE GK scores will automatically be sent to the Florida Department of Education's Bureau of Educator Certification; however to have them sent to a college or university, you must make a request when you register for the exam.

Each multiple-choice question is worth one raw point. The total number of questions you answer correctly is added up to obtain your raw score. Your raw score is then scaled. In order to pass the multiple-choice subtests, you must earn at least 200 points on each test.

Essay responses are scored on a holistic scale of 1 – 6 by two separate graders who are unaware of each other's evaluations of your work. Their scores are added together for a total of 2 – 12; if the scores differ substantially, to ensure fairness a third scorer determines your final essay score. In order to pass the Essay subtest, you must score at least 8 points.

Scores are reported either as "PASS" or "NOT PASS." If you receive even one "NOT PASS" on a subtest, you will not pass the General Knowledge Test.

Keep in mind that a small number of multiple-choice questions are experimental and will not count toward your overall score. ETS uses these to test out new questions for future exams. However, as those questions are not indicated on the test, you must respond to every question.

There is no penalty for guessing on the FTCE test, so be sure to eliminate answer choices and answer every question. If you still do not know the answer, guess; you may get it right!

How is the FTCE GK (082) Administered?

The GK is a computer-based test offered continuously at a range of universities and testing centers. It may be taken in its individual parts or all at once. Check https://home.pearsonvue.com/ for more information. You will need to print your registration ticket from your online account and bring it, along with your identification, to the testing site on test day. No pens, pencils, erasers, or calculators are allowed; on the Mathematics portion of the exam, a calculator will automatically appear on the computer screen for certain questions. You may take the test once every 31 days.

About Cirrus Test Prep

Cirrus Test Prep study guides are designed by current and former educators and are tailored to meet your needs as an incoming educator. Our guides offer all of the resources necessary to help you pass teacher certification tests across the nation.

Cirrus clouds are graceful, wispy clouds characterized by their high altitude. Just like cirrus clouds, Cirrus Test Prep's goal is to help educators "aim high" when it comes to obtaining their teacher certification and entering the classroom.

About This Guide

This guide will help you master the most important test topics and also develop critical test-taking skills. We have built features into our books to prepare you for your tests and increase your score. Along with a detailed summary of the test's format, content, and scoring, we offer an in-depth overview of the content knowledge required to pass the test. Our sidebars provide interesting information, highlight key concepts, and review content so that you can solidify your understanding of the exam's concepts. Test your knowledge with sample questions and detailed answer explanations in the text that help you think through the problems on the exam, and with two full-length practice tests that reflect the content and format of the FTCE GK. We're pleased you've chosen Cirrus to be a part of your professional journey!

1

Writing the Essay

Regardless of the format or topic, a high-scoring essay can be written by following several simple rules. First, identify the type of essay to be written: if the essay doesn't correctly address the prompt, it will always receive a low score. Second, determine what the main point and organizational structure of the essay will be. It is much easier to write using a clear outline than to haphazardly organize along the way. Third, make sure that the essay uses sound evidence while maintaining a style that's appropriate to the test. A good essay doesn't have to be complicated; it just needs to have a clear, well-reasoned position. Finally, all of this must be accomplished within a limited time frame. Fortunately, the essay graders will understand that a first draft written under test conditions does not need to be as polished as a final essay in a classroom assignment.

TYPES OF ESSAYS

It is important to note that essays do not follow a single format. Rather, the format is determined by the intended purpose of each essay. For example, an essay may attempt to inform or persuade the reader, or perhaps describe or narrate a scene. It is important to use the appropriate type of essay for a given task.

PERSUASIVE

A **persuasive essay** is meant to convince the reader of the author's point of view on a particular issue. Typically, such an essay will also include a call to action. Thus, a persuasive essay should cause the reader to feel and act in a particular way.

A persuasive essay can be written on any topic on which people can have a difference of opinion. For example, an essay may argue that social media is harmful to teenagers or that a noise ordinance should be adopted in a community. These both seek to sway the reader's opinion to that of the author's. In contrast, essays describing the social media habits of teenagers or telling the story of a neighborhood's attempt to pass local noise ordinances are not persuasive because they do not present a specific opinion.

In writing a persuasive essay, it is vital to take a clear stance on an issue. The reader should be left with no doubt as to which side of an issue the writer supports. In addition, a persuasive essay must include facts and logical reasoning to show that the ideas put forth by the author are superior to other ideas on the topic. This type of essay should be written with a specific audience in mind to tailor the arguments and language to the intended readers.

When writing persuasive essays in an exam setting, keep in mind that the actual stance taken in the essay is not important. The graders don't care about the specific opinion expressed in the essay; they only care that the opinion is well written and supported by logically relevant evidence.

PERSUASIVE ESSAY EXAMPLE

PROMPT: Technology has launched us into a new era and, with it, a new way of living with and relating to one another. It has opened doors and allowed us to accomplish things that would have been impossible in the past: we are able to keep up closely with a large number of people in an easy and comfortable way. As it continues to develop, social media technology will, time and again, offer us new and better ways of staying in touch with one another and, because of it, will make our lives and our relationships fuller and more meaningful.

Discuss the extent to which you agree or disagree with this opinion. Support your position with specific reasoning and examples from your experience, observations, and reading.

One would be foolish to argue that technology has not had a real and pervasive impact on our daily lives. Many of us rely daily on cell phones, tablets, and computers that allow us to reach family, friends, and business associates with little to no trouble. However, this ease of access does not necessarily mean our relationships are improving: the impersonal and anonymous nature of social media and other communication technologies make it even more difficult for us to make meaningful, lasting connections with the people around us.

Social media is, by nature, impersonal. Though we are able to build personal profiles that reflect whom we want the world to see, these profiles do little to improve our connection and communication with others. In fact, it is these very tools that are distancing us from our fellow humans. Birthday notifications, for example, remind social media users every day of the "friends" who are celebrating that day. While this tool seems, in theory, to be a great way to keep up with others, it actually desensitizes us. In truth, when I receive birthday notifications via social media, I end up either ignoring them altogether or sending an impersonal "Happy Birthday" just to be able to say I did. In fact, I never send birthday notes via social media to friends and family whose birthdays I actually care about because I do so in a more personal way—via a phone call or in person. Furthermore, I don't need an app to remember those birthdays. Though it may seem more useful or convenient to be able to stay in touch through social media, the relationships that rely on it are, in my experience, rarely very meaningful. By allowing us to stay in touch with larger numbers of people, social media also makes our connections shallower.

In addition to being impersonal, social media and other communication technologies can also be anonymous, creating a world of users that are disconnected from the things they post and read and, ultimately, from each other. Cyberbullying has been a significant concern of the twenty-first century, with numerous incidents leading to depressing outcomes, like teenage suicide. Through the lens of social media, bullies are able to disregard the humanity of the person on the other end and say things that they might never say in real life. A similar effect is clear during important political events: people post, with aggressive fervor, in favor of their own beliefs and respond, with equally aggressive insults, to anyone they disagree with. While this may, on the surface, seem to encourage open dialogue, social media and other communication technologies fail to have any effect on the quality of the conversation itself. Rather than learning to interact with one another respectfully, a tactic that may actually lead to increased understanding and greater acceptance of others, social media users learn that what they say has little to no consequence in real life.

The sense of community created by social media is deceptive. The ease with which people can "connect" often makes those connections meaningless. The friend who "Likes" a photo you post isn't putting any real energy into that friendship—he just clicked once and moved on. Similarly, people can use the anonymity of the internet to just as easily create enemies. One angry comment (that would never be said face-to-face) can launch a hundred nasty replies. These types of relationships don't make our lives fuller or more meaningful. They make our lives empty and shallow.

EXPOSITORY

An **expository essay** is one in which the author tells the reader something in a straightforward manner. This essay type is meant to explain, inform, or clarify a topic for which the reader may have no prior knowledge. It is also a chance for the writer to display his or her own understanding of a topic. Subjects for an expository essay might include many different sides, but an expository essay doesn't dive into these controversies. Instead, it simply explains a topic with as much neutrality as possible.

To compose a successful expository essay, the author must present facts from verifiable sources and arrange the information in a logical sequence. Language should be clear and precise, and relevant context should be provided since the reader may not be familiar with the topic. It is important that the essay remains objective and does not include the author's opinion.

> **DID YOU KNOW?**
>
> The word *expository* is related to the word *expose*, which means to show.

EXPOSITORY ESSAY EXAMPLE

PROMPT: Following the Second World War, the United States and the Soviet Union emerged as the dominant world powers, ushering in the Cold War and a "bipolar world." Only a few years before, however, European powers like England and France controlled colonial empires around the world, dominating world affairs; in fact, the Soviet Union itself was only a few decades old.

Using your knowledge of world history, explain how the two superpowers were able to rapidly dominate world affairs following World War II.

The United States and the Soviet Union—victorious allies in the Second World War—were not able to maintain a strong relationship for long. Despite losses in the millions, the Soviet Union still had an enormous and powerful military and, in violation of the agreements made at Yalta, Stalin later occupied several Eastern European countries, preventing free elections. The US-led West formed NATO as a result; in response, the USSR organized the Warsaw Pact. This rapid rise in the prominence of the United States and the USSR was a result of both countries' advanced industrial capabilities, large resource reserves, and expanded global military presence.

In the United States, the New Deal and mobilization for the war had strengthened the national economy. At the end of the war, the United States had proven its weapons capacity by using the nuclear bomb: this technology, on the heels of its military domination of Europe and the Pacific, made it an undisputed global superpower.

At the same time, the Soviet Union dominated land throughout Europe, Central, and East Asia. The Soviet Union's Five Year Plans of the 1920s had sped up industrialization, and their wealth included vast mineral, petroleum, timber, and other natural resources. They also developed nuclear weapons and a military with a global reach.

Furthermore, both countries extended their global reach diplomatically and militarily to spread their respective ideologies—communism and democratic capitalism—in order to ensure global security. By promulgating the Marshall Plan and supporting the establishment of the Bretton Woods institutions (the World Bank and the International Monetary Fund), the United States found ways to promote global capitalism. At the same time, the Soviet Union supported Marxist independence movements worldwide in colonies and resistance movements in former colonies; many Cold War battles were fought as proxy wars between the superpowers in Africa, Asia, and Latin America. Each country also had a global presence with bases, officers, diplomats, and military personnel in nearly every country in the world.

Since the European empires had collapsed in the wake of the Second World War, the Soviet Union and the United States dominated the global stage in a way no other country could match. Each used their natural and industrial resources, alongside a growing military and diplomatic presence, to quickly fill the void left by the fall of European powers.

WRITING A THESIS STATEMENT

The thesis, or **thesis statement**, is central to the structure and meaning of an essay: it presents the writer's argument or position on an issue. In other words, it tells readers specifically what the author is going to say in the essay. A strong, direct thesis statement is key to the organization of any essay. It introduces both the central idea of the essay and the main points that will be used to support that idea. Thus, the thesis will mirror the organization of the essay as a whole: each paragraph can elaborate on each supporting point.

In writing a thesis statement, it is important to respond to the prompt provided. The author must identify keywords in the prompt and think about what the prompt is asking. For example, the prompt may be asking for a clear stance to be taken a particular issue, or it may require a detailed explanation of a topic. Once a clear understanding of the task is reached, the author must develop a central idea along with supporting points from relevant sources, including any provided documents and personal knowledge or experience. The central idea and supporting points can then be concisely packaged into a one or two sentence statement. Generally, a thesis statement is no more than two sentences.

> **HELPFUL HINT**
>
> Find an op-ed article in the newspaper. Read it carefully and try to identify the thesis and supporting points.

THESIS STATEMENT EXAMPLES

PROMPT: Many high schools have begun to adopt 1:1 technology programs, meaning that each school provides every student with a computing device, such as a laptop or tablet. Educators who support these initiatives say that the technology allows for more dynamic collaboration and that students need to learn technology skills to compete in the job market. On the other hand, opponents cite increased distraction and the dangers of cyberbullying or unsupervised internet use as reasons not to provide students with such devices.

In your essay, take a position on this question. You may write about either one of the two points of view given, or you may present a different point of view on this question. Use specific reasons and examples to support your position.

Possible thesis statements:

1) Providing technology to every student is good for education because it allows students to learn important skills such as typing, web design, and video editing, and it also gives students more opportunities to work cooperatively with their classmates and teachers.

2) I disagree with the idea that schools should provide technology to students because most students will simply be distracted by the free access to games and websites when they should be studying or doing homework.

3) By providing each student with a laptop or tablet, schools can help students apply technology to work more effectively with other students, communicate with teachers and classmates, and conduct research for class projects.

STRUCTURING THE ESSAY

There are a lot of different ways to organize an essay. In the limited time frame of an exam, however, it is best to stick to a basic five-paragraph essay that includes an introduction, body, and conclusion. This structure can be used to discuss nearly any topic and will be easy for graders to follow.

INTRODUCTIONS

The purpose of an **introduction** is to set the stage for the essay. This is accomplished by capturing the reader's interest, introducing and providing context for the topic, and stating the central idea and main points of the essay. Usually the introductory paragraph ends with a thesis statement, which clearly sets forth the position or point the essay will argue.

> **INTRODUCTION EXAMPLE**
>
> **Technology has changed massively in recent years, but today's generation barely notices—high school students are already experienced with the internet, computers, apps, cameras, cell phones, and more. It's inevitable that these technologies will begin to make their way into classrooms. Opponents of 1:1 technology programs might argue that students will be distracted or misuse the technology, but that is exactly why schools must teach them to use it. Students need to know how to navigate technology safely and effectively, and schools have a responsibility to ensure they learn these skills. By providing each student with a laptop or tablet, schools can help students learn how to apply technology to work more effectively with other students, communicate with teachers and classmates, and conduct research for class projects.**
>
> **Explanation:** This introduction *introduces* the topic in the first sentence. It then provides context by discussing why technology in the classroom is an important—and controversial—topic. The paragraph closes with a thesis statement that takes a firm stance and introduces the supporting ideas that the essay will be organized around.

THE BODY PARAGRAPHS

The body of the essay should consist of two to four paragraphs, each of which is focused on a single supporting idea. The body of an essay can be organized in a number of ways:

- Body paragraphs can explain each supporting detail given in the thesis statement.
- Body paragraphs can describe a problem then discuss the pros and cons of a solution in separate paragraphs.
- Body paragraphs can tell a story, with the story broken into two to four logical parts.
- Body paragraphs can compare and contrast the merits of two arguments, possibly drawing a conclusion about which is better at the end.

Each paragraph should be structurally consistent, beginning with a topic sentence to introduce the main idea, followed by supporting ideas and examples. No extra ideas unrelated to the paragraph's focus should appear. Transition words and phrases can be used to connect body paragraphs and to improve the flow and readability of the essay.

> **QUICK REVIEW**
>
> Which essay structure would be better suited to a persuasive essay? What about an expository essay?

BODY PARAGRAPH EXAMPLE

Technology can be a powerful tool for collaboration. When all of the students in a classroom have access to reliable laptops or tablets, they are able to more effectively share information and work together on projects. Students can communicate quickly via email, share files through a cloud service, and use a shared calendar for scheduling. They also have the opportunity to teach each other new skills since each student may bring to the group unique knowledge about particular apps or programs. When the availability of technology is limited or inconsistent, these opportunities are lost.

Explanation: This body paragraph discusses a supporting detail given the thesis (*schools can help students apply technology to work more effectively with other students*). It introduces the topic, then provides concrete examples of how technology makes it easier to work with other students. The final sentence reemphasizes the paragraph's main idea.

CONCLUSIONS

To end an essay smoothly, the author must compose a conclusion that reminds the reader of the importance of the topic and then restates the essay's thesis and supporting details. The writer should revisit the ideas in the introduction and thesis statement, but these ideas should not be simply repeated word-for-word. Rather, a well-written conclusion will reinforce the argument using wording that differs from the thesis statement but conveys the same idea. The conclusion should leave the reader with a strong impression of the essay's main idea and provide the essay with a sense of closure.

CONCLUSION EXAMPLE

As technology continues to change and become more incorporated into everyday life, students will need to adapt to it. Schools already teach young people a myriad of academic and life skills, so it makes sense that they would teach students how to use technology appropriately, too. When technology is incorporated into schoolwork, students will learn to collaborate, communicate, and research more effectively. Providing students with their own devices is one part of this important task, and schools that do so should be supported.

Explanation: This conclusion reminds the reader why the topic is important and then restates the thesis and supporting ideas. It ends with a strong, clear statement of the writer's stance on the issue.

SUPPORTING EVIDENCE

An essay's arguments are made up of claims, which in turn are backed by supporting evidence. This evidence can be drawn from a number of sources. Some essay prompts will include texts from which to draw supporting evidence. Other essays will require the writer to use his or her own background knowledge of the issue. For some essay prompts, it may be appropriate to use personal anecdotes and experiences. Regardless of the source of the evidence, it is important that it be conveyed in a clear, specific, and accurate manner.

PROVIDING SPECIFIC EXAMPLES

In body paragraphs, general statements should be followed with specific examples that will help to convince the reader that the argument has merit. These specific examples do not bring new ideas to the paragraph; rather, they explain or defend the general ideas that have already been stated. A poorly written essay will be full of general claims supported by little to no evidence or specific examples. Conversely, successful essays will use multiple specific examples to back up general claims.

EXAMPLES OF GENERAL AND SPECIFIC STATEMENTS

The following are some examples of general statements, followed by examples of specific statements that provide more detailed support of an idea.

General: Students may get distracted online or access harmful websites.

Specific: Some students spend too much time using chat features or social media, or they get caught up in online games. Others spend time reading websites that have nothing to do with an assignment.

Specific: Teens often think they are hidden behind their computer screens. However, providing personal information online can lead to danger in the real world.

General: Schools can teach students how to use technology appropriately and expose them to new tools.

Specific: Schools can help students learn how to use technology to work on class projects, communicate with classmates and teachers, and carry out research for classwork.

Specific: Providing students with laptops or tablets will allow them to get lots of practice using technology and programs at home, and only school districts can ensure that these tools are distributed widely, especially to students who may not have access to them otherwise.

INCORPORATING SOURCES

Providing evidence from outside sources is an excellent way to provide support for the claims in an essay. Some essay prompts will include texts that may be cited in the essay, or writers may want to cite sources from memory. In either case, this supporting evidence should be incorporated smoothly into the essay. Context should be provided for the quote, and the quote should always be followed by a discussion of its importance or relevance to the essay.

> **HELPFUL HINT**
>
> In an essay, a quote never speaks for itself; the writer must always explain where it came from and why it is important.

When using outside sources, it is vital to credit the author or source within the text. Usually a full citation isn't needed—it can simply be sufficient to note the author's name in the text. And, as always, the writer must make sure to place direct quotations in quotation marks.

> **INCORPORATING SOURCES EXAMPLE**
>
> In addition to helping students work better with each other, technology can also help students communicate more effectively with teachers. A recent study from the University of Montana showed that over 75 percent of students have at some point been too intimidated to speak up in class, even if they thought they had something valuable to contribute (Higgins, 2015). But what if technology could provide a way to make speaking up easier? Private online messaging, comment boards for questions, and online tutorials are all made possible by introducing technology to the classroom. A well-trained teacher will be able to use these resources to encourage more effective classroom communication. In my personal experience, I have seen numerous students respond effectively when given the chance to communicate in the privacy of an online interaction.
>
> **Explanation:** This first-person paragraph incorporates two sources: a scientific study and a personal anecdote from the author.

WRITING WELL

Although the content of an essay is of primary importance, the writing itself will also factor into the essay's final score. Writing well means that the language and tone are appropriate for the purpose and audience of the essay, the flow of ideas and the relationships among them are logical and clear, and the sentences are varied enough to keep the reader interested.

Transitions

Transitions are words, phrases, and ideas that help connect ideas throughout a text both between sentences and between paragraphs. Transitions can be used to imply a range of relationships, including cause and effect, sequence, contradictions, and continuance of an idea. Consistent and creative use of transitions will help the essay flow logically from one idea to the next and will make the essay easy for the reader to follow.

> **HELPFUL HINT**
>
> Common transitions include *then, next, in other words, as well, in addition to, another, because, first, finally, in conclusion, however, in fact, therefore,* and *on the other hand.*

Transitions between paragraphs can also be polished by starting paragraphs with references to ideas mentioned in previous paragraphs or by ending them with a transition to the next topic. Such guideposts will guide the reader from one paragraph to the next.

> **EXAMPLES OF TRANSITIONS**
>
> Teens often think they are hidden behind their computer screens. <u>However,</u> providing personal information online can lead to danger in the real world.
>
> <u>In addition to</u> helping students work better with each other, technology can also help students communicate more effectively with teachers.
>
> They <u>also</u> have the opportunity to teach each other new skills.

Syntax

A variety of well-written sentences will help maintain the reader's interest in the essay. To create this theme, a writer can use sentences that differ in length and that begin with varying words, rather than repeating the same word at the start of each new sentence. It is also important for the writer to use a mix of different sentence structures, including simple, complex, compound, and compound-complex sentences.

> **SYNTAX EXAMPLE**
>
> **Technology can be a powerful tool for collaboration. When all of the students in a classroom have access to reliable laptops or tablets, they are able to more effectively share information and work together on projects. Students can communicate quickly via email, share files through a cloud service, and use a shared calendar for scheduling. They also have the opportunity to teach each other new skills since each student may bring to the group unique knowledge about particular apps or programs. When the availability of technology is limited or inconsistent, these opportunities are lost.**

Explanation: This paragraph starts with a short, simple sentence and follows with a longer, more complex sentence. The next sentence is also long, but it is a simple sentence with a single clause. The second-to-last sentence is complicated with multiple clauses, but it is immediately followed with a short, easy-to-read statement that ends the paragraph.

WORD CHOICE AND TONE

The words a writer chooses influence the reader's assessment of the essay. When writing essays, it is always necessary to choose words that are appropriate to the task.

For instance, a formal essay on an academic topic may benefit from complex sentences and an expansive vocabulary. However, a first-person essay on a personal topic may use a more causal vocabulary and organization. In general, when writing for exam graders, it is best to use clear, direct vocabulary and avoid using vague, general words such as good, bad, very, or a lot. Showing variety in word choice can also help improve an essay's score. However, it is better to use more familiar vocabulary than to try to impress the exam grader with unfamiliar words or words that do not fit the context of the essay.

WORD CHOICE EXAMPLES

Technology has changed massively in recent years, but today's generation barely notices—high school students are already experienced with the internet, computers, apps, cameras, cell phones, and more. It is inevitable that these technologies will be begin to make their way into classrooms. Opponents of 1:1 technology programs might argue that students will be distracted or misuse the technology, but that is exactly why schools must teach them to use it. Students need to know how to navigate technology safely and effectively, and schools have a responsibility to ensure they learn these skills. By providing each student with a laptop or tablet, schools can help students apply technology to work more effectively with other students, communicate with teachers and classmates, and conduct research for class projects.

Technology is everywhere in modern life. We've all walked into a coffee shop full of laptops or have seen people walking with their phones in front of their faces. I know I've often looked up from my tablet to realize I've missed a whole conversation. With technology everywhere, it seems obvious that we would start using it in classrooms. Opponents of 1:1 technology programs say that technology will be too distracting or will be abused by students, but it seems like that's an even more important reason for students to learn how to use it. Schools are where students learn all kinds of life skills, and technology is just another skill to learn. By giving students laptops or tablets, schools can help students work better with each other, work better with teachers, and learn to do better research.

Explanation: The two paragraphs above discuss the same topic. The first has a word choice and tone for an academic essay; the second is written in a more relaxed, personal style.

Managing Time

When working on an essay under time constraints, it is important to manage time wisely. Simply launching into the introduction will likely result in a hurried, unorganized essay and a low score. Instead, the writer should take a few minutes to plan.

As a first step, the writer should thoroughly read the prompt and any accompanying texts, and then determine the type of essay that is required. Next, the writer must decide on a thesis and what kind of supporting evidence to use. Once the thesis is clear, it is a good idea for the writer to create a brief outline of the essay. This whole process should only take a few minutes, leaving the bulk of the time for writing. However, it is always a good idea to leave a few minutes at the end to proofread and revise as necessary.

> **HELPFUL HINT**
>
> Underline key words in the prompt so you can refer to them while writing the essay. This can help keep you and your essay focused.

Example Essays

PROMPT: The rise in popularity of e-cigarettes has reduced the overall smoking rate according to the Centers for Disease Control and Prevention. Many hail the new technology for helping smokers quit traditional tobacco cigarettes. However, others raise concerns about the appeal of e-cigarettes to young people and advocate FDA regulation of e-cigarettes to prevent negative side effects of their use on a new generation of smokers.

In your essay, take a position on this question. You may write about either one of the two points of view given, or you may present a different point of view on this question. Use specific reasons and examples to support your position.

> **EXAMPLE ESSAY ONE**
>
> For decades, youth smoking was a major concern for both parents and public health advocates. With education campaigns informing youth of the dangers of smoking and legal action taken against tobacco producers for their advertising tactics, the number of youth smoking traditional cigarettes has never been lower. But new technology is threatening to overturn that progress as electronic (e-cigarettes) have skyrocketed in popularity among both adults and youth. E-cigarettes should be regulated by the FDA to prevent youth from smoking since the long-term effects of e-cig use are unknown, youth are still becoming addicted to nicotine, and e-cigs could be a gateway to traditional smoking.
>
> Smoking has long been a way for young people to feel cool or sophisticated. Popular culture, including film and television, glamorized smoking and led generations of Americans to pick up the habit. Although traditional smoking is no longer considered cool, the use of e-cigarettes, or vaping, threatens to take the same position in popular culture. Companies

which produce traditional cigarettes have long been banned from advertising their products on television, but because e-cigarettes are not regulated by the FDA, there are no restrictions on their advertisement. This allows e-cig companies to reach youth through a wide range of media. Furthermore, the gadget-like design of e-cigs and the variety of candy-like flavors make them especially appealing to youth—a tactic that seems designed to hook a new generation on smoking.

This is particularly concerning as the long-term effects of vaping are not yet known for either adults or youth. The technology is too new to have been studied adequately. The FDA must study a drug for years before it can become available to the general public. Yet a device that delivers a highly-addictive substance remains unregulated. It is true that e-cigarettes are healthier for smokers than traditional cigarettes, but we cannot yet know the impact on youth who would have otherwise not smoked but for the easy access to these drug-delivery devices.

In addition, we do know that nicotine is a highly addictive drug and that once this habit is established, it is very difficult to quit. If nothing else, this is a wasteful way for young people to spend their money. But even more concerning is the danger that nicotine use could alter the brain chemistry of young people and potentially make them prone to other addictions. Even if vaping does not become a gateway to hard drug use, it does make the leap to traditional smoking much more likely, and we know how harmful cigarettes have been.

The FDA has a responsibility to protect the public's health, and it is clear that regulation is needed to stop the momentum of the e-cigarette industry from getting youth addicted to their products. Although long-term health effects of vaping are unknown at this time, we must be cautious and err on the side of safety. At the very least, youth can be spared from an expensive, addictive habit; at best, an entire generation can live longer, healthier lives.

Explanation: This response provides good context for the discussion of the topic and takes a clear stance on the issue raised in the prompt. Strong examples and sound reasoning support the thesis. The essay is cohesive, and strong transitions connect ideas. Vocabulary and tone are appropriate, and the conclusion leaves the reader with a sense of the importance of the issue. Overall, this response would receive a high score.

EXAMPLE ESSAY TWO

Everyone knows smoking is bad for you. So, it's good that lots of people are quitting, and I think e-cigarettes, or vapes as they are also called, are helping people quit. Even though I don't use them, I know some people who use vapes, and they seem pretty healthy. It may be true that e-cigarettes have harmful side-effects, but it will be too far into the future before we know. The FDA should be studying this so that we do know if vapes are safe to use, especially for kids. No one wants kids to get hooked on drugs or to be unhealthy.

If they do start smoking, it is better for the kids to use e-cigarettes. They are less harmful because they don't use real tobacco or produce the terrible smelling smoke that normal cigarettes do. Some of my friends vape, and I don't even mind being in the same room. They actually smell pretty sweet. I don't think it's good to vape too much, but once in a while is fine, and I hope people make good choices about smoking.

Explanation: This response does not sufficiently address the prompt. The writer seems to disagree with the position of FDA regulation of e-cigarettes but does not develop this into a clear thesis. The writer's position is further confused by stating that the FDA should be studying the matter. The response is short and lacks adequate supporting detail. Although some personal examples are used, they are weak and a divergence from the main point. Although free of most errors, the language is simplistic, personal pronouns are overused, and the tone is not appropriate for academic writing. Overall, this response would receive a low score.

English Language Skills

PARTS OF SPEECH

The **parts of speech** are the building blocks of sentences, paragraphs, and entire texts. There are eight parts of speech: nouns, pronouns, verbs, adverbs, adjectives, conjunctions, prepositions, and interjections. Each plays a unique role in a sentence.

The exam tests the reader's ability to identify errors in sentences. Readers will need a basic knowledge of the parts of speech to answer these questions correctly.

NOUNS AND PRONOUNS

Nouns give names to people, places, things, and ideas. Nouns are usually the subject or object in a sentence.

There are several types of nouns: common nouns ("chair," "car," "house"), proper nouns ("Julie," "David"), abstract nouns ("love," "intelligence," "sadness"), concrete nouns ("window," "bread," "person"), compound nouns ("brother-in-law," "roller coaster"), non-countable nouns ("money," "water"), countable nouns ("dollars," "cubes"), and verbal nouns ("writing," "diving").

> **HELPFUL HINT**
>
> The subject performs the action of a sentence, while the object has the action performed on it.

In the following sentence, there are three nouns: "family," "cabin," and "lake":

> The <u>family</u> visited the <u>cabin</u> by the <u>lake</u>.

Writers use **pronouns** to replace nouns in a sentence or paragraph to avoid repetition. The noun that a pronoun replaces is called its **antecedent**.

Pronouns fall into several categories. Some of the basic types of pronouns are listed in Table 2.1.

Table 2.1. Pronouns

Pronoun Type	Purpose	Example
Personal pronouns	act as subjects or objects in a sentence	She received a letter; I gave the letter to her.
Possessive pronouns	indicate possession	My coat is red; our car is blue.
Reflexive pronouns	intensify or reflect back on a noun	I myself made the dessert. I made the dessert myself.

Personal, possessive, and reflexive pronouns must agree with the noun they replace in gender (male, female, or neutral), number (singular or plural), and person.

Person refers to the point of view. First person is the point of view of the speaker ("I," "me"), second person is the person being addressed ("you"), and third person refers to a person outside the sentence ("he," "she," "they").

Table 2.2. Personal, Possessive, and Reflexive Pronouns

Case	First Person		Second Person		Third Person	
	singular	*plural*	*singular*	*plural*	*singular*	*plural*
Subject	I	we	you	you (all)	he, she, it	they
Object	me	us	you	you (all)	him, her, it	them
Possessive	my	our	your	your	his, her, its	their
Reflexive	myself	ourselves	yourself	yourselves	himself, herself, itself	themselves

Table 2.3. Indefinite Pronouns

Singular		Plural	Singular or Plural
each	everybody	both	some
either	nobody	few	any
neither	somebody	several	none
one	anybody	many	all
everyone	everything		most
no one	nothing		more
someone	something		
anyone	anything		
	another		

Indefinite pronouns replace nouns to avoid unnecessary repetition:

> My friend asked me to choose between two dresses, but I like both.

Indefinite pronouns can be singular or plural (and some can act as both, depending on the context). If the indefinite pronoun is the subject of the sentence, it is important to know whether that pronoun is singular or plural so the verb can agree with the pronoun in number.

SAMPLE QUESTIONS

1) Which pronoun correctly completes the sentence?

   My wife taught me to drive stick shift so ___ could use her car while mine was in the shop.

   A. you
   B. I
   C. my
   D. his

2) Which pronoun correctly completes the sentence?

   _____ believes that going to a party the night before your certification exam is a bad idea.

   A. Everybody
   B. Something
   C. Several
   D. Few

VERBS

Verbs express action ("run," "jump," "play") or state of being ("is," "seems"). Verbs can stand alone, or they can be accompanied by **helping verbs**, which are used to indicate tense.

HELPFUL HINT

Helping verbs include: is, am, are, was, were; be, being, been; has, had, have; do, does, did; should, would, could; will

Verb tense indicates the time of the action. The action may have occurred in the past, may be occurring in the present, or might occur in the future. The action may also have been simple (occurring once) or continuous (ongoing). The perfect and perfect continuous tenses describe when actions occur in relation to other actions.

Table 2.4. Verb Tenses

Tense	Past	Present	Future
Simple	I answered the question.	I answer your questions in class.	I will answer your question.
Continuous	I was answering your question when you interrupted me.	I am answering your question; please listen.	I will be answering your question after the lecture.

Table 2.4. Verb Tenses (continued)

Tense	Past	Present	Future
Perfect	I had answered all questions before class ended.	I have answered the questions already.	I will have answered every question before the class is over.
Perfect continuous	I had been answering questions when the students started leaving.	I have been answering questions for thirty minutes and am getting tired.	I will have been answering students' questions for twenty years by the time I retire.

Changing the spelling of a verb and/or adding helping verbs is called **conjugation**. In addition to tense, verbs are conjugated to indicate *person* (first, second, and third) and *number* (singular or plural).

The conjugation of the verb must agree with the subject of the sentence. A verb that has not been conjugated is called an infinitive and begins with "to" ("to swim," "to be").

Table 2.5. Verb Conjugation (Present Tense)

Person	Singular	Plural
First person	I answer	we answer
Second person	you answer	you (all) answer
Third person	he/she/it answers	they answer

> **HELPFUL HINT**
>
> A noun that receives the direct object is the indirect object: "The pitcher will throw Antoine the ball."

Finally, verbs can be classified by whether they take a **direct object**, a noun that receives the action of the verb. **Transitive verbs** require a direct object. In the sentence below, the transitive verb "throw" has a direct object (the ball):

The pitcher will throw the ball.

Intransitive verbs do not require a direct object. Verbs like "run," "jump," and "go" make sense without any object:

He will run.

She jumped.

Many sets of similar verbs include one transitive and one intransitive verb, which can cause confusion. Some troublesome verb combinations include lie/

lay, rise/raise, and sit/set. The exam may test on these. Some commonly confused intransitive and transitive verbs are listed in the table below.

Table 2.6. Intransitive and Transitive Verbs

Intransitive Verbs	Transitive Verbs
lie: to recline	lay: to put (lay something)
rise: to go or get up	raise: to lift (raise something)
sit: to be seated	set: to put (set something)
Hint: These intransitive verbs have *i* as the second letter. "Intransitive" begins with *i*.	Hint: The word "transitive" begins with a *t*, and it *TAKES* an object.

SAMPLE QUESTIONS

3) Choose the correctly conjugated verb to complete the sentence.

   By this time tomorrow, I _____ my exam.

   A. finish
   B. will finish
   C. will have finished
   D. had finished

4) Which sentence contains an error?

   A. Please sit the plate down on the table.
   B. She lay the towel on the sand at the beach.
   C. Students should raise their hands if they have a question.
   D. Every morning, the sun rises.

ADJECTIVES AND ADVERBS

Adjectives modify, or describe, nouns and pronouns. In English, adjectives are usually placed before the word being modified, although they can also come after a linking verb such as "is" or "smells":

The beautiful blue jade necklace will go perfectly with my dress.

I think that lasagna smells delicious.

The suffixes *–er* and *–est* are used to modify adjectives in a comparison. The suffix *–er* is used when comparing two things, and the suffix *–est* is used when comparing more than two:

Anne is taller than Steve, but Steve is more coordinated.

> Of the five brothers, Jordan is the <u>funniest</u>, and Alex is the <u>most intelligent</u>.

Adjectives longer than two syllables are compared using "more" (for two things) or "most" (for three or more things):

> **Incorrect**: Of my <u>two</u> friends, Clara is <u>the smartest</u>.

> **Correct**: Of my <u>two</u> friends, Clara is <u>smarter</u>.

"More" and "most" should not be used with –*er* and –*est* endings:

> **Incorrect**: My <u>most warmest</u> sweater is made of wool.

> **Correct**: My <u>warmest</u> sweater is made of wool.

Adverbs, which are often formed by adding the suffix –*ly*, modify any word (or set of words) that is not a noun or pronoun:

> He quickly ran to the house next door. ("Quickly" modifies the verb "ran.")

> Her very effective speech earned her a promotion. ("Very" modifies the adjective "effective.")

HELPFUL HINT

Adverbs typically answer the questions Where? When? Why? How? How often? To what extent? Under what conditions?

SAMPLE QUESTION

5) Which of the following sentences contains an adjective error?
    A. The new red car was faster than the old blue car.
    B. Reggie's apartment is in the tallest building on the block.
    C. The slice of cake was tastier than the brownie.
    D. Of the four speeches, Jerry's was the most long.

CONJUNCTIONS

Conjunctions join words into phrases, clauses, and sentences. There are three main types of conjunctions: coordinating, correlative, and subordinating.

Coordinating conjunctions join together two independent clauses (i.e., two complete thoughts). These include "for," "and," "nor," "but," "or," "yet," "so" (the acronym FANBOYS can help you remember these words). Note that some of these can also be used to join items in a series:

> I will order lunch, <u>but</u> you need to go pick it up.

Make sure to get sandwiches, chips, and sodas.

Correlative conjunctions (whether/or, either/or, neither/nor, both/and, not only/but also) work together to join items:

Both the teacher and the students needed a break
after the lecture.

When connecting two subjects with correlative conjunctions, the second one must agree with the verb that follows:

Incorrect: I will neither mow the grass nor do I want
to pull weeds today.

Correct: I will neither mow the grass nor pull the weeds today.

Subordinating conjunctions join dependent clauses (thoughts that cannot stand alone as sentences) to the related independent clause. They usually describe a relationship between the two parts of the sentence, such as cause-effect or order. They can appear at the beginning or in the middle of a sentence:

> **HELPFUL HINT**
>
> The exam does not test the names of the different conjunctions, but it will test on sentence errors caused by misused conjunctions.

We treat ourselves during football season to several orders
because we love pizza.

Because we love pizza, we treat ourselves during football season
to several orders.

SAMPLE QUESTION

6) **Which sentence contains an error?**
    A. I don't know whether I'll be available tomorrow.
    B. Although she was cold, she hesitated before turning off the air-conditioning.
    C. Neither my mother nor my father has been to Canada.
    D. Because I was hungry and didn't bring any lunch.

PREPOSITIONS

Prepositions set up relationships in time ("after the party") or space ("under the cushions") in a sentence. A preposition will always function as part of a prepositional phrase, which includes the preposition and the object of the preposition:

I ran over the river and through the woods.

In the above example, the prepositions are "over" and "through." The prepositional phrases are "over the river" and "through the woods."

Table 2.7. Common Prepositions

Prepositions	Compound Prepositions
along, among, around, at, before, behind, below, beneath, beside, besides, between, beyond, by, despite, down, during, except, for, from, in, into, near, of, off, on, onto, out, outside, over, past, since, through, till, to, toward, under, underneath, until, up, upon, with, within, without	according to, as of, as well as, aside from, because of, by means of, in addition to, in front of, in place of, in respect to, in spite of, instead of, on account of, out of, prior to, with regard to

Interjections, words like "hey" or "wow" are parts of speech. They have no grammatical attachment to the sentence other than to add expressions of emotion. They may be punctuated with commas or exclamation points and may appear anywhere in a sentence: "<u>Ouch</u>! He stepped on my toe."

> **SAMPLE QUESTION**
>
> 7) Which preposition correctly completes this sentence?
>
> I threw the ball _____ my friend.
>
> A. among
> B. since
> C. during
> D. to

CONSTRUCTING SENTENCES

In English, words are used to build phrases and clauses. These are then combined to create sentences. Phrases and clauses are made up of a subject, a predicate, or both.

The **subject** is what the sentence is about. It is usually a noun that performs the main action of the sentence, and it may be accompanied by modifiers. The **predicate** describes what the subject is doing or being. It contains the verb(s) and any modifiers or objects that accompany it.

On the exam, you will need to identify errors in sentence structure, including sentence fragments, poorly constructed sentences, run-on sentences, dangling modifiers, and more.

PHRASES

A **phrase** is a group of words that communicates a partial idea and lacks either a subject or a predicate. Phrases are categorized based on the main word in the phrase.

A **prepositional phrase** (discussed above) begins with a preposition and ends with an object of the preposition:

> The dog is hiding under the porch.

A **verb phrase** is composed of the main verb and its helping verbs:

> The chef would have created another soufflé,
> but the staff protested.

A **noun phrase** consists of a noun and its modifiers:

> The big, red barn rests beside the vacant chicken house.

When looking for grammatical errors on the exam, test takers should be alert for questions that include phrases masquerading as sentences. A long, complicated phrase can be confused for a complete sentence ("The enthusiastic new student in the class with the blue sweatshirt and the blonde hair"). Remember: a sentence always has a subject and a predicate; a phrase will have only one of those.

SAMPLE QUESTION

8) Which of the following contains an error?
   A. Ten cats in a row.
   B. My teacher was late today.
   C. All applicants participate.
   D. Clouds fill the sky.

CLAUSES

Clauses contain both a subject and a predicate. They can be either independent or dependent. An **independent** (or main) **clause** can stand alone as its own sentence:

> The dog ate her homework.

Dependent (or subordinate) **clauses** cannot stand alone as their own sentences. They start with a subordinating conjunction, relative pronoun, or relative adjective, which will make them sound incomplete:

> Because the dog ate her homework

Table 2.8. Words That Begin Dependent Clauses

Subordinating Conjunctions	Pronouns and Adjectives
after, although, as, because, before, even if, even though, if, in order that, once, provided, since, so, so that, than, that, though, unless, until, when, whenever, where, whereas, wherever, whether, while	how, that, when, where, which, who, whoever, whom, whomever, whose, why

SAMPLE QUESTION

9) Which of the following contains an error?
   A. I watch TV while I knit.
   B. She called me before she left.
   C. You ate more than he did.
   D. Whenever I visit her.

COMPOSING A SENTENCE

Every sentence needs at least one independent clause. For example, the following independent clause is a complete sentence:

> The cat jumped.

There is a subject, "cat," and a verb, "jumped."

Other elements, like phrases and clauses, can be added:

> The cat jumped onto the porch.

In the above sentence, the subject is "The cat," the verb is "jumped," and a prepositional phrase has been added for context: "onto the porch."

Additional clauses can be added. As sentences become more complicated, writers may need to use punctuation or conjunctions (see "Conjunctions" and "Punctuation" in this chapter for more information):

> The cat jumped onto the porch; it then walked into the house.

> The cat jumped onto the porch, and it looked in the window.

In the above sentences, an independent clause has been joined to the original sentence. In the first sentence, the independent clause "it then walked into the house" is connected with a semicolon. In the second sentence, the independent clause "it looked in the window" is connected with the coordinating conjunction "and" and a comma.

To link a dependent clause, commas may or may not be required, depending on context. Commas are discussed in more detail below (see "Punctuation"):

> The cat jumped onto the porch because it wanted to get out of the rain.

The clause "because it wanted to get out of the rain" cannot stand on its own. It must be connected to an independent clause.

Questions on the exam may ask about errors in sentence structure. For example, you may be asked to identify the error in a compound sentence in which the independent clauses are connected incorrectly.

> **SAMPLE QUESTION**
>
> 10) Which of the following would be the BEST way to write the underlined portion of the sentence?
>
>   While these incidents sometimes end in funny or heartwarming <u>stories at</u> other times they end in fear and destruction.
>
>   A. stories, at
>   B. stories; at
>   C. stories: at
>   D. stories—at

PUNCTUATION

The main **punctuation marks** are periods, question marks, exclamation marks, colons, semicolons, commas, quotation marks, and apostrophes.

There are three terminal punctuation marks used to end sentences.

- The **period** ends declarative (statement) and imperative (command) sentences.
- The **question mark** ends interrogative sentences.
- **Exclamation marks** indicate that the writer or speaker is exhibiting intense emotion or energy.

> Sarah and I are attending a concert.

> How many people are attending the concert?

> What a great show that was!

The **colon** and the **semicolon**, though often confused, have a unique set of rules about their respective uses. While both punctuation marks are used to join clauses, the construction of the clauses and the relationship between them is different.

The **semicolon** is used to show a general relationship between two independent clauses (IC; IC):

> The disgruntled customer tapped angrily on the counter; she had to wait nearly ten minutes to speak to the manager.

Coordinating conjunctions (*FANBOYS*, discussed on page 20) cannot be used with semicolons. However, conjunctive adverbs can be used following a semicolon:

> She may not have to take the course this year; however, she will eventually have to sign up for that specific course.

The **colon**, somewhat less limited than the semicolon in its usage, is used to introduce a list, a definition, or a clarification. The clause preceding the colon must be an independent clause, but the clause that follows does not have to be:

> **Incorrect**: The buffet offers three choices that include: ham, turkey, or roast.

> **Correct**: The buffet offers three choices: ham, turkey, or roast.

> **Correct**: The buffet offers three choices that include the following: ham, turkey, or roast.

Note that neither the semicolon nor the colon should be used to set off an introductory phrase from the rest of the sentence:

> **Incorrect**: After the trip to the raceway; we realized that we should have brought earplugs.

> **Incorrect**: After the trip to the raceway: we realized that we should have brought earplugs.

> **Correct**: After the trip to the raceway, we realized that we should have brought earplugs.

The **comma** is a complicated type of punctuation that can serve many different purposes in a sentence. Comma placement is often an issue of style, not mechanics, meaning there may not be only one correct way to write the sentence. There are, however, a few important hard-and-fast comma rules.

1. Commas should be used to separate two independent clauses along with a coordinating conjunction:

   > Khalid ordered the steak, but Bruce preferred the ham.

2. Commas should be used to separate coordinate adjectives (two different adjectives that describe the same noun):

   > The shiny, regal horse ran majestically through the wide, open field.

3. Commas should be used to separate items in a series. The comma before the conjunction is called the Oxford, or serial, comma. (It is optional and will not appear on the exam.)

   > The list of groceries included cream, coffee, donuts, and tea.

4. Commas should be used to separate introductory words, phrases, and clauses from the rest of the sentence:

> <u>Slowly,</u> Nathan became aware of his surroundings after the concussion.
>
> <u>Within an hour,</u> the authorities will descend on the home.
>
> <u>After Alice swam the channel,</u> nothing intimidated her.

5. Commas should be used to set off appositive phrases: descriptors that are not needed for the sentence to make sense grammatically:

> Estelle<u>, our newly elected chairperson,</u> will be in attendance.
>
> Ida<u>, my neighbor,</u> watched the children for me last week.

6. Commas should be used to set off titles of famous individuals:

> Charles<u>, Prince of Wales,</u> visited Canada several times in the last ten years.

7. Commas should be used to set off the day and month of a date:

> I was born on <u>February 16, 1958,</u> in Minnesota.

8. Commas should be used in numbers of more than four digits:

> We expect <u>25,000</u> visitors to the new museum.

Quotation marks are used for many purposes. They are used to enclose direct quotations in a sentence. Terminal punctuation that is part of the quotation goes inside the marks, and terminal punctuation that is part of the larger sentence goes outside:

> She asked him menacingly, "Where is my peanut butter?"
>
> What is the original meaning of the phrase "king of the hill"?

In American English, commas are used to set quotations apart from the surrounding text and are placed inside the marks:

> "Although I find him tolerable," Arianna wrote, "I would never want him as a roommate."

Additionally, quotation marks enclose titles of short, or relatively short, literary works such as short stories, chapters, and poems (titles of longer works, like novels and anthologies, are italicized):

> For English class, we read "The Raven" by Edgar Allan Poe.

Writers also use quotation marks to set off words used in a special sense or for a nonliterary purpose:

> The shady dealings of his Ponzi scheme earned him the ironic name "Honest Abe."

Apostrophes (sometimes referred to as single quotation marks) have a number of different uses:

- show possession
- replace missing letters, numerals, and signs
- form plurals of letters, numerals, and signs in certain instances

1. To signify possession by a singular noun not ending in *s*, add *'s*:

    boy → boy's

2. To signify possession by a singular noun ending in *s*, add *'s*:

    class → class's

3. To signify possession by an indefinite pronoun not ending in *s*, add *'s*:

    someone → someone's

4. To signify possession by a plural noun not ending in *s*, add *'s*:

    children → children's

5. To signify possession by a plural noun ending in *s*, add only the apostrophe:

    boys → boys'

6. To signify possession by singular, compound words and phrases, add *'s* to the last word in the phrase:

    everybody else → everybody else's

7. To signify joint possession, add *'s* only to the last noun:

    John and Mary's house

8. To signify individual possession, add *'s* to each noun:

    John's and Mary's houses

9. To signify missing letters in a contraction, place the apostrophe where the letters are missing:

    do not → don't

10. To signify missing numerals, place the apostrophe where the numerals are missing:

    1989 → '89

11. There are differing schools of thought regarding the pluralization of numerals and dates, but writers should use one style consistently within the document:

> 1990's/1990s; A's/As

SAMPLE QUESTIONS

11) Which of the following is the correct version of the underlined portion of the sentence below?

    Fred's brother wanted the following items for <u>Christmas a</u> red car, a condo, and a puppy.
    - A. Christmas; a
    - B. Christmas, a
    - C. Christmas. A
    - D. Christmas: a

12) Which of the following sentences contains a comma usage error?
    - A. On her way home she stopped to pick up groceries, pay her electric bill, and buy some flowers.
    - B. I used to drink coffee every morning but my office took away the coffee machine.
    - C. Elizabeth will order the cake for the party after she orders the hats.
    - D. My cousin, who lives in Indiana, is coming to visit this weekend.

CAPITALIZATION

Capitalization questions will ask about errors in capitalization within a phrase or sentence. Below are the most important rules for capitalization.

The first word of a sentence is always capitalized:

> We will be having dinner at a new restaurant tonight.

The first letter of a proper noun is always capitalized:

> We're going to Chicago on Wednesday.

Titles are capitalized if they precede the name they modify:

> Joe Biden, the vice president, met with President Obama.

Months are capitalized, but not the names of the seasons:

> Snow fell in March even though winter was over.

The names of major holidays should be capitalized. The word "day" is only capitalized if it is part of the holiday's name:

> We always go to a parade on Memorial Day, but Christmas day we stay home.

The names of specific places should always be capitalized. General location terms are not capitalized:

> We're going to San Francisco next weekend so I can see the ocean.

Titles for relatives should be capitalized when they precede a name, but not when they stand alone:

> Fred, my uncle, will make fried chicken, and Aunt Betty is going to make spaghetti.

SAMPLE QUESTION

13) Which of the following sentences contains a capitalization error?
    A. My two brothers are going to New Orleans for Mardi Gras.
    B. On Friday we voted to elect a new class president.
    C. Janet wants to go to Mexico this Spring.
    D. Peter complimented the chef on his cooking.

AVOIDING COMMON USAGE ERRORS

Some of the most common grammatical errors are those involving agreement between subjects and verbs, and between nouns and pronouns. While it is impossible to cover all possible errors, the lists below include the most common agreement rules to look for on the test.

ERRORS IN SUBJECT-VERB AGREEMENT

Test takers will be asked to find errors in subject-verb agreement on the exam. To prepare for these questions, practice identifying the subject and the verb in a sentence and review the rules for subject-verb agreement.

1. Single subjects agree with single verbs; plural subjects agree with plural verbs:

    > The <u>girl walks</u> her dog.

    > The <u>girls walk</u> their dogs.

2. Compound subjects joined by "and" typically take a plural verb unless considered one item:

    > <u>Correctness and precision are required</u> for all good writing.

Macaroni and cheese makes a great snack for children.

3. Compound subjects joined by "or" or "nor" agree with the nearer or nearest subject:

Neither I nor my friends are looking forward to our final exams.

Neither my friends nor I am looking forward to our final exams.

4. For sentences with inverted word order, the verb will agree with the subject that follows it:

Where are Bob and his friends going?

Where is Bob going?

5. All single, indefinite pronouns agree with single verbs:

Neither of the students is happy about the play.

Each of the many cars is on the grass.

Every one of the administrators speaks highly of Trevor.

6. All plural, indefinite pronouns agree with plural verbs:

Several of the students are happy about the play.

Both of the cars are on the grass.

Many of the administrators speak highly of Trevor.

7. Collective nouns agree with singular verbs when the collective acts as one unit. Collective nouns agree with plural verbs when the collective acts as individuals within the group:

The band plans a party after the final football game.

The band play their instruments even if it rains.

The jury announces its decision after sequestration.

The jury make phone calls during their break time.

8. Nouns that are plural in form but singular in meaning will agree with singular verbs:

Measles is a painful disease.

Sixty dollars is too much to pay for that book.

9. Singular verbs come after titles, business names, and words used as terms:

"Three Little Kittens" is a favorite nursery rhyme for many children.

General Motors is a major employer for the city.

Ignore words between the subject and the verb to help make conjugation clearer:

The new library with its many books and rooms fills a long-felt need.

SAMPLE QUESTION

14) Which sentence does NOT contain an error?
    A. My sister and my best friend lives in Chicago.
    B. My parents or my brother is going to pick me up from the airport.
    C. Neither of the students refuse to take the exam.
    D. The team were playing a great game until the rain started.

PRONOUN-ANTECEDENT AGREEMENT AND PRONOUN ERRORS

Pronoun errors are commonly tested on the exam. Below are some of the more common pronoun rules that may appear on the test.

1. The antecedent and pronoun must agree in gender and number:

    I baked a cake for my mother because it was her birthday.

2. Antecedents joined by "and" require a plural pronoun:

    The children and their dogs enjoyed their day at the beach.

3. For antecedents joined by "or," the pronoun agrees with the nearest antecedent:

    Either the resident mice or the manager's cat gets itself a meal of good leftovers.

4. The pronoun must agree with the number of the indefinite pronouns:

    Neither student finished her assignment.

    Both of the students finished their assignments.

5. When "each" and "every" precede the antecedent, the pronoun should be singular:

    Each child brings unique qualities to his or her family.

    Every writer is attending his or her assigned lecture.

6. If a pronoun leads to ambiguity, do not use it:

My mom and my sister went to pick up my sister's new phone. (not "her new phone")

David and Henry lost David's wallet in the park. (not "his wallet")

SAMPLE QUESTION

15) Which sentence does NOT contain an error?
    A. The grandchildren and their cousins enjoyed their day at the beach.
    B. Most of the grass has lost their deep color.
    C. The jury was cheering as their commitment came to a close.
    D. Every boy and girl must learn to behave themselves in school.

MODIFIER ERRORS

Adjectives, adverbs, and **modifying phrases** (groups of words that together modify another word) should be placed as close as possible to the word they modify. Separating words from their modifiers can create incorrect or confusing sentences:

Incorrect: Running through the hall, the bell rang, and the student knew she was late.

Correct: Running through the hall, the student heard the bell ring and knew she was late.

Who is running: the bell or the student? The phrase "running through the hall" should be placed next to "student," the noun it modifies. The modifier error in the incorrect sentence is a **dangling modifier**. The modifier is "dangling" in the sentence separately from what it is modifying. This is a common error tested on the exam.

SAMPLE QUESTION

16) Which of the following sentences contains a structural error?
    A. Adult penguins are black and white, but penguin chicks are gray.
    B. Being allergic to bananas, smoothies were not Donna's preferred breakfast.
    C. Each unit is scheduled for periodic maintenance when winter is over.
    D. Sometimes I lie on the floor and read by the fire, or I sit on the couch and watch TV.

ERRORS IN SENTENCE CONSTRUCTION

Errors in parallelism occur when items in a series are not put in the same form. For example, if a list contains two nouns and a verb, the sentence should be rewritten so that all three items are the same part of speech. Parallelism should be maintained in words, phrases, and clauses:

> The walls were painted <u>green</u> and <u>gold</u>.

> Her home is <u>up the hill</u> and <u>beyond the trees</u>.

> <u>If we shop on Friday</u> and <u>if we have enough time</u>, we will then visit the aquarium.

Sentence errors fall into three categories: fragments, comma splices (comma fault), and fused sentences (run-on). A **fragment** occurs when a group of words lacks both a subject and verb as needed to construct a complete sentence or thought:

> **Incorrect**: Why am I not going to the mall? Because I do not like shopping.

> **Correct**: Because I do not like shopping, I will not plan to go to the mall.

A **comma splice** (comma fault) occurs when two independent clauses are joined together with only a comma to "splice" them together. To fix a comma splice, add a coordinating conjunction or replace the comma with a semicolon:

> **Incorrect**: My family eats turkey at Thanksgiving, we eat ham at Christmas.

> **Correct**: My family eats turkey at Thanksgiving, and we eat ham at Christmas.

> **Correct**: My family eats turkey at Thanksgiving; we eat ham at Christmas.

Fused (run-on) sentences occur when two independent clauses are joined with no punctuation. Like comma splices, they can be fixed with a comma and conjunction or with a semicolon:

> **Incorrect**: My sister lives nearby she never comes to visit.

> **Correct**: My sister lives nearby, but she never comes to visit.

> **Correct**: My sister lives nearby; she never comes to visit.

English Language Skills

SAMPLE QUESTIONS

17) Which of the following would NOT be an acceptable way to revise and combine the underlined portion of these sentences?

    They receive an <u>annual pension payment. The amount of the pension</u> has been reviewed and changed a number of times.

    A. annual pension payment, the amount of which
    B. annual pension payment; the amount of the pension
    C. annual pension payment; over the years since 1958, the amount of the pension
    D. annual pension payment, the amount of the pension

18) Which of the following contains an error in sentence structure?
    A. I asked the teacher when the project was due; she said we had two weeks to finish it.
    B. I love running, to swim, and also going hiking, but I hate camping.
    C. Most of my friends enjoy soccer, but I prefer basketball.
    D. The municipal government stated that there would be no budget increase this year.

19) Which of the following sentences contains a comma splice?
    A. Since she went to the store.
    B. The football game ended in a tie, the underdog caught up in the fourth quarter.
    C. If we get rid of the bookcase, we'll have enough room for a couch.
    D. When the players dropped their gloves, a fight broke out on the ice hockey rink floor.

WORDINESS AND REDUNDANCY

A sentence may be grammatically correct but still confusing because the writer has repeated words or ideas for no logical reason. In some forms of writing, repetition is purposeful. However, the exam tests a candidate's knowledge of clear and concise writing.

The exam will ask you to clarify wordy sentences or remove redundant phrasing (when several words with similar meanings are used).

Some examples of excessive wordiness and redundancy include:

▶ A memo was sent out <u>concerning the matter of</u> dishes left in the sink. →
   A memo was sent out <u>about</u> dishes left in the sink.

▶ The email was <u>brief and to the point</u>. → The email was <u>terse</u>.

▶ I don't think I'll ever <u>understand or comprehend</u> Italian operas. →
   I don't think I'll ever <u>understand</u> Italian operas.

> **SAMPLE QUESTION**
>
> 20) What is the BEST way to revise this redundant sentence?
>
> **It was an unexpected surprise to see you this weekend.**
>
> A. It was a surprise to see you this weekend; we didn't expect it!
> B. Seeing you this weekend was a surprise!
> C. We didn't expect to see you this weekend, it was a surprise.
> D. To be seeing you this weekend, it surprised us.

COMMONLY CONFUSED WORDS

The exam may feature questions about usage and correct word choice. The list below gives some common sets of words that are often misused. These fall into three general categories:

1. Homophones: words sound the same but have different meanings (e.g., "insure" and "ensure")
2. Words with related but distinct meanings (e.g., "amount" and "number")
3. Related words that function as different parts of speech (e.g., "good" and "well")

  ▷ **a, an**: "A" is used before words beginning with consonants or consonant sounds. "An" is used before words beginning with vowels or vowel sounds.

  ▷ **affect, effect**: "Affect" is most often a verb; "effect" is usually a noun. ("The experience affected me significantly" or "The experience had a significant effect on me.")

  ▷ **among, amongst, between**: "Among" is used for a group of more than two people. "Amongst" is archaic and not commonly used in modern writing. "Between" is reserved to distinguish two people, places, things, or groups.

  ▷ **amount, number**: "Amount" is used for non-countable sums; "number" is used with countable nouns. ("She had a large amount of money in her purse, nearly fifty dollars.")

  ▷ **cite, site**: "Cite" is a verb used in documentation to credit an author of a quotation, paraphrase, or summary. "Site" is a location.

  ▷ **elicit, illicit**: "Elicit" means to draw out a response from an audience or a listener. "Illicit" refers to illegal activity.

  ▷ **every day, everyday**: "Every day" is an indefinite adjective modifying a noun—"each day" could be used interchangeably with "every day." "Everyday" is a one-word adjective to describe frequent occurrence. ("Our visit to the Minnesota State Fair is an everyday activity during August.")

  ▷ **fewer, less**: "Fewer" is used with a countable noun; "less" is used with a non-countable noun. ("Fewer parents are experiencing stress since the new teacher was hired" or "Parents are experiencing <u>less</u> stress since the new teacher was hired.")

- **firstly, secondly**: These words are archaic. Today, "first" and "second" are more commonly used.
- **good, well**: "Good" is always the adjective; "well" is always the adverb except in cases of health. ("She felt <u>well</u> after the surgery.")
- **implied, inferred**: "Implied" is something a speaker does; "inferred" is something the listener does after assessing the speaker's message. ("The speaker <u>implied</u> something mysterious, but I <u>inferred</u> the wrong thing.")
- **irregardless, regardless**: "Irregardless" is nonstandard usage and should be avoided. "Regardless" is the proper usage of the transitional statement.
- **its, it's**: "Its" is a possessive case pronoun. "It's" is a contraction for "it is."
- **moral, morale**: "Moral" is a summative lesson from a story or life event. "Morale" is the emotional attitude of a person or group of people.
- **principal, principle**: "Principal" is the leader of a school in the noun usage. "Principal" means *main* in the adjectival usage. "Principle" is also a noun meaning *idea* or *tenet*. ("The <u>principal</u> of the school spoke on the <u>principal</u> meaning of the main <u>principles</u> of the school.")
- **quote, quotation**: "Quote" is a verb and should be used as a verb. "Quotation" is the noun and should be used as a noun.
- **reason why**: "Reason why" is a redundant expression—use one or the other. ("The <u>reason</u> we left is a secret" or "<u>Why</u> we left is a secret.")
- **should of, should have**: "Should of" is improper usage, likely resulting from misunderstood speech—"of" is not a helping verb and therefore cannot complete the verb phrase. "Should have" is the proper usage. ("He <u>should have</u> driven.")
- **than, then**: "Than" sets up a comparison of some kind. "Then" indicates a reference to a point in time. ("When I said I liked the hat better <u>than</u> the gloves, my sister laughed; <u>then</u> she bought both for me.")
- **their, there, they're**: "Their" is the possessive case of the pronoun "they." "There" is a demonstrative pronoun indicating location, or place. "They're" is a contraction of the words "they are," the third-person plural subject pronoun and third-person plural, present-tense conjugation of the verb "to be." These words are very commonly confused in written English.

▷ **to lie (to recline), to lay (to place)**: "To lie" is the intransitive verb meaning "to recline," so the verb does not take an object. "To lay" is the transitive verb meaning "to place something." ("I <u>lie</u> out in the sun; I <u>lay</u> my towel on the beach.")

▷ **to try and**: "To try and" is sometimes used incorrectly in place of "to try to." ("She should <u>try to</u> succeed daily.")

▷ **unique**: "Unique" is an ultimate superlative. The word "unique" should not be modified technically. ("The experience was <u>unique</u>" not "The experience was <u>very unique</u>.")

▷ **who, whom**: "Who" is a subject-relative pronoun. ("My son, <u>who is</u> a good student, studies hard.") Here, the son is carrying out the action of studying, so the pronoun is a subject pronoun ("who"). "Whom" is the object relative pronoun. ("My son, <u>whom</u> the other students admire, studies hard.") Here, "son" is the object of the other students' admiration, so the pronoun standing in for "him," "whom," is an object pronoun.

▷ **your, you're**: "Your" is the possessive case of the pronoun "you." "You're" is a contraction of the words "you are," the second-person subject pronoun and the second-person singular, present-tense conjugation of the verb "to be." These words are commonly confused in written English.

SAMPLE QUESTION

21) **Identify the error in the following sentence.**

    We should have known that the principal reason for the decline in exports was the affect of economic sanctions.

    A. should have
    B. principal
    C. reason
    D. affect

Answer Key

1) A. Incorrect. The pronoun "you" does not make sense here. It is the writer's car that is in the shop, not a different person.

   B. **Correct.** The pronoun "I" refers to the writer. It agrees with the verb "could use." The pronouns "me" and "mine" also refer to the writer, so first-person singular makes the most sense.

   C. Incorrect. "My" is a possessive pronoun. It cannot function as the subject of a verb (here, "could use").

   D. Incorrect. "His" is a possessive pronoun. It cannot act as the subject of a verb. It also does not make sense in this sentence.

2) A. **Correct.** The singular indefinite pronoun "everybody" agrees with the singular verb "believes" and makes sense in this sentence.

   B. Incorrect. The indefinite pronoun "something" does agree in number with the singular verb "believes," but it does not make sense in the sentence.

   C. Incorrect. The singular verb "believes" does not agree with the plural pronoun "several."

   D. Incorrect. The plural indefinite pronoun "few" does not agree with the singular verb "believes."

3) C. **Correct.** This sentence requires the future perfect tense because the speaker is talking about an event that will be conducted and completed in the future.

4) A. **Correct.** The intransitive verb "sit" is used incorrectly here. The writer should have used the transitive verb "set," which means "to put" or "to set something" down, like plates on a table.

5) D. **Correct.** Choice D should read "Of the four speeches, Jerry's was the longest." The word "long" has only one syllable, so it should be modified with the suffix –est, not the word "most."

6) D. **Correct.** This is a sentence fragment that begins with the subordinating conjunction "because." There is no independent clause.

7) D. **Correct.** Prepositions establish relationships in space (or time). This sentence describes a spatial relationship, so it needs a preposition about space or direction. The preposition "to" clarifies the relationship between the speaker, the ball, and the speaker's friend: the speaker is throwing the ball *to* the friend.

8) A. **Correct.** This choice is not a complete sentence. Rather, it is a combination of two phrases: a noun phrase ("Ten cats") and a prepositional phrase ("in a row"). There is no verb and no predicate.

9) D. **Correct.** This is a sentence fragment. It is a dependent clause beginning with a subordinating conjunction, "whenever." It contains a subject, "I,"

and a predicate, "visit," but there is no independent clause attached to the dependent clause. Therefore, it cannot act as a full sentence.

10) **A.** **Correct.** The first clause is dependent and the second is independent, so they are correctly joined by a comma.

11) **D.** **Correct.** A colon can be used to introduce a list.

12) **B.** **Correct.** This compound sentence requires a comma before the conjunction "but."

13) **C.** **Correct.** "Spring" is the name of a season and should not be capitalized.

14) **B.** **Correct.** The verb agrees with the closest subject—in this case, the singular "brother."

15) **A.** **Correct.** "Grandchildren" and "cousins" are plural and so take the plural pronoun "their."

16) **B.** **Correct.** This sentence contains a dangling modifier. Who is allergic to bananas? Probably Donna, but "smoothies" appears next to the modifying phase "being allergic to bananas." The writer probably means that Donna is allergic to bananas, but this sentence is written in a confusing manner and contains a structural error.

17) **D.** **Correct.** This choice creates a comma splice. The other choices are all correct.

18) **B.** **Correct.** This sentence does not use parallel structure. A better version would be "I love running, swimming, and hiking, but I hate camping."

19) A. Incorrect. This group of words is not a complete thought and would be considered a fragment.

   B. **Correct.** This sentence joins two complete thoughts with only a comma and would therefore be classified as a comma splice.

   C. Incorrect. This sentence correctly joins a dependent and independent clause using a comma.

   D. Incorrect. This sentence is punctuated properly and constructed correctly.

20) A. Incorrect. This sentence is still redundant; a surprise is, by definition, unexpected.

   B. **Correct.** This concise rewrite expresses the idea without any redundancy or grammatical errors.

   C. Incorrect. This choice contains both redundancy and a grammatical error (a comma splice).

   D. Incorrect. This sentence is clumsy. It is needlessly wordy, though there is no redundancy.

21) **D.** **Correct.** The word "affect" is used incorrectly here. The correct usage is "effect."

Reading Skills

INTRODUCTION

The Reading Test assesses overall proficiency in several key reading skills, including building inferences, understanding themes, and describing the organization and craft of writing.

The test has forty multiple-choice questions. Questions follow a brief passage of text or media, such as a graph. The number of questions following each passage depends on how long the passage is: four to seven questions follow a 200-word passage or a pair of passages; three questions follow a 100-word passage; and single questions follow statements and briefer passages. Question stems may appear as fill-in-the-blank sentences, straightforward questions, or *LEAST/NEVER/EXCEPT* questions, which ask the reader to choose the answer that does not fit.

The FTCE Reading Test has three main question categories based on the Common Core State Standards. Several strategies and terms are discussed in the following sections and throughout this book.

KEY IDEAS AND DETAILS

This category focuses on the text as a whole. The questions ask for explanations of the main ideas and how they lead to inferences and conclusions. Look for connections between sections of the text as well as consistency and meaning of the author's argument. Test takers should also identify and accurately summarize the theme by giving details that support the author's argument.

Strategies for approaching this type of question include previewing the questions and outlining. Reading through the questions before reading the passage is a good way for students to find a focus. The questions describe what to look for, and students can rule out wrong answer choices by finding the main ideas and supporting details. Students can outline the text by jotting down words or phrases that describe the main idea of each paragraph and underlining important details that support that idea.

Craft, Structure, and Language Skills

This category tests understanding of the craft of writing. This includes the use of language, point of view, and organization. Questions may require relating the details of a passage to the overall organization and meaning of that passage. These questions ask for evaluations of specific areas of the text as they relate to the author's purpose and argument, and descriptions of how the author uses specific words, figurative language, or transitions.

For these craft-related questions, the best strategy entails returning to the passage after reading each question and looking for the specific context and location of each question. Marking wrong answers and circling the important aspects of the question stem and answer are also helpful strategies.

Integrating Information and Ideas

This final category combines the strategies used with the other two categories. The synthesis of these skills extends into evaluation and judgment.

Questions may require an assessment of a text, a comparison of multiple texts, or an examination of other kinds of texts, such as visual media. To compare two texts, for example, the test taker must understand the purpose and main idea of each text as well as specific details. Determining what to pay attention to is accomplished by reviewing each question before reading its relative passage and returning to the passage as needed. A passage with media such as visuals requires the same skills as reading text. Readers should consider each question to determine the skills and knowledge needed to answer it. Deconstructing the question stem reveals what sort of question it is.

The Main Idea

Identifying the Main Idea

The main idea of a text is the argument the author is making about a particular topic. Every sentence in a passage should support or address the main idea in some way. To identify the main idea, first identify the topic. The difference between the two is simple: the **topic** is the overall subject matter of a passage; the **main idea** is what the author wants to say about that topic.

Consider a political election. A candidate is running for office and plans to deliver a speech asserting her position on tax reform, which is that taxes should be lowered. The topic of the speech is tax reform, and the main idea is that taxes should be lowered. The candidate is going to say this in her speech and support it with examples proving why lowering taxes would benefit the public and how it could be accomplished.

Other candidates may have different perspectives on the same topic. They may think higher taxes are necessary or current taxes are adequate. Their speeches, while on the same topic of tax reform, would probably have different main ideas supported by different examples and evidence.

> **HELPFUL HINT**
>
> **Topic**: the subject of the passage. **Main idea**: the argument the writer is making about the topic.

Read the following passage and identify the topic and main idea.

> Babe Didrikson Zaharias, one of the most decorated female athletes of the twentieth century, is an inspiration for everyone. Born in 1911 in Beaumont, Texas, Zaharias lived in a time when women were considered second class to men, but she never let that stop her from becoming a champion. Zaharias was one of seven children in a poor immigrant family and was competitive from an early age. As a child she excelled at most things she tried, especially sports, which continued into high school and beyond. After high school, Zaharias played amateur basketball for two years, and soon after began training in track and field. Despite the fact that women were only allowed to enter in three events, Zaharias represented the United States in the 1932 Los Angeles Olympics, and won two gold medals and one silver in track and field events.

The topic of this paragraph is obviously Babe Zaharias—the whole passage describes events from her life. Determining the main idea, however, requires a little more analysis. To figure out the main idea, ask what the writer is saying about Zaharias. The writer describes Zaharias as an inspiration and talks about the hardships she overcame and her many accomplishments. These details support the writer's main idea: Babe Zaharias is an accomplished and inspirational woman.

Fictional works may have a theme instead of a main idea. A **theme** is an idea or perspective that emerges from the way a literary work engages with its topic. For example, a central topic in F. Scott Fitzgerald's novel *The Great Gatsby* is money: the characters are all defined by their relative wealth. The theme of the novel is what Fitzgerald is trying to say about money: that being extremely wealthy leads to excess and moral decay.

SAMPLE QUESTIONS

The Battle of the Little Bighorn, commonly called Custer's Last Stand, was a battle between the Lakota, the Northern Cheyenne, the Arapaho, and the Seventh Cavalry Regiment of the US Army. Led by war leaders Crazy Horse and Chief Gall and the religious leader Sitting Bull, the allied tribes of the Plains Indians decisively defeated their US foes. Two hundred and sixty-eight US soldiers were killed, including General George Armstrong Custer, two of his brothers, his nephew, his brother-in-law, and six Indian scouts.

1) **What is the main idea of this passage?**
    A. Most of General Custer's family died in the Battle of the Little Bighorn.
    B. Crazy Horse and Chief Gall were important leaders of the Plains Indians.
    C. The Seventh Cavalry Regiment was formed to fight Native American tribes.
    D. The Battle of the Little Bighorn was a significant victory for the Plains Indians.

In 1953, doctors surgically removed the hippocampus of patient Henry Molaison in an attempt to stop his frequent seizures. Unexpectedly, he lost the ability to form new memories, leading to the biggest breakthrough in the science of memory. Molaison's long-term memory—of events more than a year before his surgery—was unchanged, as was his ability to learn physical skills. From this, scientists learned that different types of memory are handled by different parts of the brain, with the hippocampus responsible for *episodic memory*, the short-term recall of events. They have since discovered that some memories are then channeled to the cortex, the outer layers of the brain that handle higher functions, where they are gradually integrated with related information to build lasting knowledge about our world.

2) **The main idea of the passage is that**
    A. Molaison's surgery posed significant risk to the functioning of his brain.
    B. short-term and long-term memory are stored in different parts of the brain.
    C. long-term memory forms over a longer period than short-term memory.
    D. memories of physical skills are processed differently than memories of events.

TOPIC AND SUMMARY SENTENCES

The topic, and sometimes the main idea of a paragraph, is introduced in the **topic sentence**. The topic sentence usually appears early in a passage. The first sentence in the paragraph about Babe Zaharias states the topic and main idea: "Babe Didrikson Zaharias, one of the most decorated female athletes of the twentieth century, is an inspiration for everyone."

Even though paragraphs generally begin with topic sentences, writers sometimes build up to the topic sentence by using supporting details to generate interest or build an argument. Readers should watch out for paragraphs that do not include a clear topic sentence.

The **summary sentence**, on the other hand, often—but not always—comes at the end of a paragraph or passage, because it wraps up all the ideas presented. This sentence provides an understanding of what the author wants to say about the topic and what conclusions to draw about it.

The topic sentence acts as an introduction to a topic, allowing readers to activate their own ideas and experiences. The summary statement asks readers to accept the author's ideas about that topic. A summary sentence helps readers quickly identify a piece's main idea.

> **SAMPLE QUESTIONS**
>
> The Constitution of the United States establishes a series of limits to rein in centralized power. "Separation of powers" distributes federal authority among three branches: the executive, the legislative, and the judicial. The system of "checks and balances" prevents any one branch from usurping power. "States' rights" are protected under the Constitution from too much encroachment by the federal government. "Enumeration of powers" names the specific and few powers the federal government has. These four restrictions have helped sustain the American republic for over two centuries.
>
> 3) Which of the following is the passage's topic sentence?
>   A. These four restrictions have helped sustain the American republic for over two centuries.
>   B. The Constitution of the United States establishes a series of limits to rein in centralized power.
>   C. "Enumeration of powers" names the specific and few powers the federal government has.
>   D. The system of "checks and balances" prevents any one branch from usurping power.
>
> 4) Which of the following is the passage's summary sentence?
>   A. These four restrictions have helped sustain the American republic for over two centuries.
>   B. The Constitution of the United States establishes a series of limits to rein in centralized power.
>   C. "Enumeration of powers" names the specific and few powers the federal government has.
>   D. The system of "checks and balances" prevents any one branch from usurping power.

SUPPORTING DETAILS

The middle of a paragraph is built with **supporting details**. Supporting details come in many forms. The purpose of the passage dictates the type of details that will support the main idea. A persuasive passage may use facts and data or give specific reasons for the author's opinion. An informative passage will mostly use facts about the topic to support the main idea. Even a narrative passage will have supporting details—specific things the author says to develop the story and characters.

The most important aspect of supporting details is that they support the main idea. Examining supporting details and how they work together will help readers understand the author's view on a topic and the passage's main idea. Supporting details are key to understanding a passage.

How can readers identify the most important information in a passage? Supporting details help pinpoint the main idea, but it is easier to first locate the most important supporting details by understanding the main idea. This way, the pieces that make up the main argument become clear.

Let's look again at the passage about athlete Babe Zaharias.

> Babe Didrikson Zaharias, one of the most decorated female athletes of the twentieth century, is an inspiration for everyone. Born in 1911 in Beaumont, Texas, Zaharias lived in a time when women were considered second class to men, but she never let that stop her from becoming a champion. Babe was one of seven children in a poor immigrant family and was competitive from an early age. As a child she excelled at most things she tried, especially sports, which continued into high school and beyond. After high school, Babe played amateur basketball for two years, and soon after began training in track and field. Despite the fact that women were only allowed to enter in three events, Zaharias represented the United States in the 1932 Los Angeles Olympics, and won two gold medals and one silver for track and field events.

The main idea is that Zaharias is someone to admire—an idea introduced in the opening sentence. The rest of the paragraph gives details that support this idea. These details include the circumstances of her childhood, her early success at sports, and the medals she won at the Olympics.

Readers looking for supporting details should watch for signal words. **Signal words** are transitions and conjunctions that explain how one sentence or idea is connected to another. They "signal" that a supporting fact or idea will follow, and so can be helpful in identifying supporting details. These words and phrases can be anywhere in a sentence. Signal words can add information, provide counterarguments, create organization in a passage, or draw conclusions. Some common signal words are "in particular," "in addition," "besides," "in contrast," "therefore," and "because."

Signal words can also help rule out certain sentences as the main idea or topic sentence. If a sentence begins with one of these phrases, it will likely be too specific to be a main idea.

Readers can use supporting details to understand the main idea of a text or support an argument, but they must evaluate these details for relevance and consistency. The author might leave out details that do not directly support the main idea of a text or that support an opposing argument. Readers should think critically about what information authors choose to include or leave out. This is particularly important in persuasive writing, when an author's bias may influence their writing.

Critical reading means being alert for striking features of a text. For example, does a description seem exaggerated or overstated? Do certain words—such as "agonizing"—seem overly emotive? Are rhetorical questions used to lead the reader to a certain conclusion? Bias and audience are discussed later in this chapter (see "Understanding the Author" on page 50).

SAMPLE QUESTIONS

For thirteen years, a spacecraft called *Cassini* was on an exploratory mission to Saturn. The spacecraft was designed not to return but to end its journey by diving into Saturn's atmosphere. This dramatic ending provided scientists with unprecedented information about Saturn's atmosphere and its magnetic and gravitational fields. First, however, *Cassini* passed Saturn's largest moon, Titan, where it recorded data on Titan's curious methane lakes, gathering information about potential seasons on the planet-sized moon. Then it passed through the unexplored region between Saturn itself and its famous rings. Scientists hope to learn how old the rings are and to directly examine the particles that make them up. *Cassini*'s mission ended in 2017, but researchers have new questions for future exploration.

5) According to the passage, scientists want to learn more about Titan's
   A. gravity, based on examination of its magnetic field.
   B. rings, based on the particles that compose them.
   C. seasons, based on changes to its lakes.
   D. age, based on analysis of its minerals and gases.

The study showed that private tutoring gives a significant advantage to those students who are able to afford it. Researchers looked at the grades of students who had received free tutoring through the school versus those whose parents had paid for private tutors. The study included 2500 students in three high schools across four grade levels. The study found that private tutoring corresponded with a rise in grade point average (GPA) of 0.5 compared to students who used the school's free tutor service, and 0.7 compared to students who used no tutoring. After reviewing the study, the board is recommending that the school restructure its free tutor service to provide a more equitable education for all students.

6) Which of the following would weaken the author's argument?
   A. the fact that the cited study was funded by a company that provides discounted tutoring through schools
   B. a study showing differences in standardized test scores between students at schools in different neighborhoods
   C. a statement signed by local teachers stating that they do not provide preferential treatment in the classroom or when grading
   D. a study showing that GPA does not strongly correlate with success in college

Facts and Opinions

A **fact** is a piece of information that can be proven true or false. Its truthfulness or falsity cannot be changed, no matter who verifies it. The statement "Wednesday comes after Tuesday" is a fact—anyone can point to a calendar to prove it. An **opinion** is a belief that others may or may not agree with. The assertion "Television is more entertaining than feature films" is an opinion—people will agree or disagree with this statement, and there is no reference to prove or disprove it.

Authors use both facts and opinions as supporting details. They may mix facts with opinions or state an opinion as if it were a fact. The exam may ask readers to differentiate between facts and opinions.

> **QUICK REVIEW**
>
> Choose the phrase that signals an opinion: "for example," "studies have shown," "I believe," "in fact," "it is possible that."

> **SAMPLE QUESTION**
>
> The most important part of brewing coffee is getting the right water. Choose a water that you think has a nice, neutral flavor. Anything with too many minerals or contaminants will change the flavor of the coffee, and water with too few minerals won't do a good job of extracting the flavor from the coffee beans. Water should be heated to between 195 and 205 degrees Fahrenheit. Boiling water (212 degrees Fahrenheit) will burn the beans and give your coffee a scorched flavor.
>
> While the water is heating, grind your beans. Remember, the fresher the grind, the fresher the flavor of the coffee. The number of beans depends on your personal taste. Obviously, more beans will result in a more robust flavor, while fewer beans will give your coffee a more subtle taste. The texture of the grind should not be too fine (which can lead to bitter coffee) or too coarse (which can lead to weak coffee).
>
> Once the beans are ground and the water has reached the perfect temperature, you're ready to brew. A French press (which we recommend) allows you to control brewing time and provide a thorough brew. Pour the grounds into the press, then pour the hot water over the grounds and let it steep. The brew shouldn't require more than five minutes, although if you like your coffee a bit harsher, you can leave it longer. Finally, use the plunger to remove the grounds and pour.
>
> 7) Which of the following statements based on the passage should be considered an opinion?
>
>   A. While the water is heating, grind your beans.
>
>   B. A French press (which we recommend) allows you to control brewing time and provide a thorough brew.
>
>   C. Anything with too many minerals or contaminants will change the flavor of the coffee, and water with too few minerals won't do a good job of extracting the flavor from the coffee beans.
>
>   D. Finally, use the plunger to remove the grounds and pour.

MAKING INFERENCES

In addition to understanding the main idea and factual content of a passage, readers should think about other information in a passage. In a nonfiction passage, for example, questions might ask which statement the author would agree with. In a fictional work, readers might be asked to anticipate what a character would do next.

To answer such questions, readers need to understand the topic and main idea of the passage. This information allows the reader to figure out which of the answer choices best fits the criteria (or, alternatively, which do not).

Readers should try to understand the explicit meanings of information or a narrative. This happens when they draw conclusions and make logical inferences. To draw a conclusion, readers consider the details or facts. They then come to a **conclusion**—the next logical point in the thought sequence.

For example, in a Hemingway story, an old man sits alone in a café. A young waiter says that the café is closing, but the old man continues to drink. The waiter starts closing up, and the old man signals for a refill. Based on these details, the reader might conclude that the old man has not understood the waiter's desire for him to leave.

> **HELPFUL HINT**
>
> Readers draw conclusions by thinking about how the author wants them to feel. Some carefully selected facts can cause readers to feel a certain way.

An inference is different from a conclusion. An **inference** is an assumption the reader makes based on details in the text as well as their own knowledge. It is more of an educated guess that extends the literal meaning. Inferences begin with the given details. The reader then uses these to figure out more facts. What the reader already knows informs what is suggested by the details of decisions or situations in the text. In the example above, the reader might infer that the old man is lonely, enjoys being in the café, and is reluctant to leave.

It is important to infer character motivation when reading fictional text. The characters' actions move the plot forward. A series of events is understood by making sense of why the characters did what they did. Hemingway includes contrasting details as the young waiter and an older waiter discuss the old man. The older waiter sympathizes with the old man. Both men have no one at home and experience a sense of emptiness in life, which brings them to the café.

> **DID YOU KNOW?**
>
> When considering a character's motivations, the reader should ask what the character wants to achieve, what the character will get by accomplishing this, and what the character seems to value the most.

Another aspect of understanding text is connecting it to other texts. Readers may connect the Hemingway story about the old man in the café to other Hemingway stories about people dealing with loss and loneliness in a dignified way. They can extend their initial connections to people they know or their personal experiences.

When readers read a persuasive text, they often connect the arguments made to counterarguments and opposing evidence of which they are aware. They use these connections to infer meaning.

> **SAMPLE QUESTIONS**
>
> Between November 15 and December 21, 1864, Major General William Tecumseh Sherman marched Union troops from the recently captured city of Atlanta to the port of Savannah. The goal was not only to capture the port city and secure Georgia for the Union but also to destroy the Confederacy's infrastructure and demoralize its people. Sherman and his troops destroyed rail lines and burned buildings and fields. They packed only twenty days' worth of rations, foraging for the rest of their supplies from farms along the way. By the time they reached Savannah, they had destroyed 300 miles of railroad and countless cotton gins and mills, and seized 4000 mules, 13,000 head of cattle, 9.5 million pounds of corn, and 10.5 million pounds of fodder. Sherman estimated his troops inflicted $100 million in damages.
>
> 8) It can be inferred from the passage that the Confederacy
>   A. strongly resisted the actions of Sherman's troops.
>   B. was greatly weakened by the destruction.
>   C. used the march as a rallying point.
>   D. was relatively unaffected by the march.

The cisco, a foot-long freshwater fish native to the Great Lakes, once thrived throughout the basin but had virtually disappeared by the 1950s. Today, however, fishermen are pulling them up by the net-load in Lake Michigan and Lake Ontario. It is highly unusual for a native species to revive, and the reason for the cisco's reemergence is even more unlikely. The cisco have an invasive species, quagga mussels, to thank for their return. Quagga mussels depleted nutrients in the lakes, harming other species highly dependent on these nutrients. Cisco, however, thrive in low-nutrient environments. As other species—many invasive—diminished, cisco flourished in their place.

9) It can be inferred from the passage that most invasive species
   A. support the growth of native species.
   B. do not impact the development of native species.
   C. struggle to survive in their new environments.
   D. cause the decline of native species.

UNDERSTANDING THE AUTHOR

Many questions on the FTCE Reading Test will ask readers to interpret an author's intentions and ideas. This means readers must examine the author's perspective and purpose as well as the way the author uses language to communicate these things.

In every passage, an author chooses words, structures, and content with specific purpose and intent. With this in mind, the reader can understand why an author picks certain words and structures and how these relate to the content.

THE AUTHOR'S PURPOSE

The author sets out with a specific goal: to communicate a particular idea to an audience. The **author's purpose** is determined by asking why the author wants the reader to understand the passage's main idea. There are four purposes an author might have:

- to entertain the reader
- to persuade the reader of an opinion or argument
- to describe something, such as a person, place, thing, or event
- to explain a process or procedure

Within each of these general purposes, the author may direct the audience to take a clear action or respond in a certain way.

Identifying an author's purpose can be tricky, but the writing itself often gives clues. For example, if an author's purpose is to entertain, the writing may include vivid characters, exciting plot twists, or beautiful, figurative language. On the other hand, if an author wishes to persuade the reader, there may be an argument or convincing examples that support the author's point of view. An author who wishes to describe a person, place, or event may include lots of details as well as plenty of adjectives and adverbs. Finally, the author whose purpose is to explain a process or procedure may include step-by-step instructions or information in a sequence.

There are different **modes** of written materials that are related to an author's purpose. A short story, for example, is meant to entertain, while an online news article is designed to inform the public about a current event. Each type of writing has a specific name:

- Narrative writing tells a story (novel, short story, play).
- Informational or expository writing informs people (newspaper and magazine articles).
- Technical writing explains something (product manual, instructions).
- Persuasive writing tries to convince the reader of something (opinion column or a blog).

The author's purpose for writing a passage is also connected to the structure of that text. In a **narrative**, the author tells a story to illustrate a theme or idea the reader needs to consider. In a narrative, the author uses characteristics of storytelling, such as chronological order, characters, and a defined setting, and these characteristics communicate the author's theme or main idea.

In an **expository** passage, on the other hand, the author simply seeks to explain an idea or topic to the reader. The main idea will probably be a factual statement or a direct assertion of a broadly held opinion. Expository writing can come in many forms, but one essential feature is a fair and balanced representation of a topic. The author may explore one detailed aspect or a broad range of characteristics, but he or she mainly seeks to prompt a decision from the reader.

Similarly, in **technical** writing, the author's purpose is to explain specific processes, techniques, or equipment so the reader can use that process or equipment to get a desired result. Writing like this uses chronological or spatial structures, specialized vocabulary, and imperative or directive language.

> **TEACHING TIP**
>
> When reading a persuasive text, students should be aware of what the author believes about the topic.

In **persuasive** writing, the author seeks to convince the reader to accept an opinion or belief. Much like expository writing, persuasive writing is presented in many organizational forms, but the author uses specific techniques, or **rhetorical strategies**, to build an argument. Readers can identify these strategies to clearly understand what an author wants them to believe, how the author's perspective and purpose may lead to bias, and whether the passage includes any logical fallacies.

Common rhetorical strategies include the appeals to ethos, logos, and pathos. An author uses these to build trust with the reader, to explain the logical points of their argument, and to convince the reader to agree with their opinion.

An **ethos—ethical—appeal** uses balanced, fair language and seeks to build a trusting relationship between the author and the reader. An author might explain their credentials, include the reader in an argument, or offer concessions to an opposing argument.

A **logos—logical—appeal** builds on that trust by providing facts and support for the author's opinion, explaining the argument with clear connections and reasoning. At this point, the reader should beware of logical fallacies that connect unrelated ideas and build arguments on faulty premises. With a logical appeal, an author tries to convince the reader to accept an opinion or belief by showing that not only is it the most logical option, but it also satisfies the reader's emotional reaction to a topic.

A **pathos—emotional—appeal** does not depend on reasonable connections between ideas. Instead, it reminds the reader, through imagery, strong language, and personal connections, that the author's argument aligns with the reader's best interests.

Many persuasive passages use all three rhetorical strategies to appeal to the reader.

Clues will help the reader determine many things about a passage, from the author's purpose to the passage's main idea, but understanding an author's purpose is essential to fully understanding the text.

SAMPLE QUESTIONS

The Gatling gun, a forerunner of the modern machine gun, was an early rapid-fire spring-loaded, hand-cranked weapon. In 1861, Dr. Richard J. Gatling designed the gun to allow one person to fire many shots quickly. His goal was to reduce the death toll of war by decreasing the number of soldiers needed to fight. The gun had a central shaft surrounded by six rotating barrels. A soldier turned a crank, which rotated the shaft. As each barrel reached a particular point in the cycle, it fired, ejected its spent cartridge, and loaded another. During this process, it cooled down, preparing it to fire again. The Gatling gun was first used in combat by the Union Army during the Civil War. However, each gun was purchased directly by individual commanders. The US Army did not purchase a Gatling gun until 1866.

10) The primary purpose of the passage is to
- A. explain why the Gatling gun was harmful to troops.
- B. critique the US Army's use of the Gatling gun.
- C. describe the design and early history of the Gatling gun.
- D. analyze the success of Dr. Gatling in achieving his goals.

The greatest changes in sensory, motor, and perceptual development happen in the first two years of life. When babies are first born, most of their senses operate in a similar way to those of adults. For example, babies are able to hear before they are born. Studies show that babies turn toward the sound of their mothers' voices just minutes after being born, indicating they recognize the mother's voice from their time in the womb.

The exception to this is vision. A baby's vision changes significantly in the first year of life. Infants initially have a range of vision of only 8 – 12 inches and no depth perception. As a result, they rely primarily on hearing. Vision does not become the dominant sense until babies are around twelve months old. Babies prefer faces to other objects. This preference, along with their limited vision range, means that their sight is initially focused on their caregiver.

11) Which of the following best describes the mode of the passage?
- A. expository
- B. narrative
- C. persuasive
- D. descriptive

TEXT STRUCTURE

The structure of a text determines how the reader understands the argument and how the various details interact to form the argument. Authors can structure passages in several different ways. These distinct organizational patterns, referred to as **text structure**, use the logical relationships between ideas to improve the readability and coherence of a text. The most common ways passages are organized are:

- ▸ **problem-solution**: The author outlines a problem and then discusses a solution.

- **comparison-contrast**: The author presents two situations and then discusses the similarities and differences.
- **cause-effect**: The author recounts an action and then discusses the resulting effects.
- **descriptive**: The author describes an idea, object, person, or other item in detail.
- **chronological**: The author describes a situation or tells a story in chronological order.

> **HELPFUL HINT**
>
> Authors often use repetition to reinforce an idea, including repeated words, phrases, or images.

When analyzing a text, the reader should consider how text structure influences the author's meaning. Most important, the reader needs to be aware of how an author emphasizes an idea by the way he or she presents information. For example, including a contrasting idea makes a central idea stand out, and including a series of concrete examples creates a force of facts to support an argument.

SAMPLE QUESTION

The greatest changes in sensory, motor, and perceptual development happen in the first two years of life. When babies are first born, most of their senses operate in a similar way to those of adults. For example, babies are able to hear before they are born. Studies show that babies turn toward the sound of their mothers' voices just minutes after being born, indicating they recognize the mother's voice from their time in the womb.

The exception to this is vision. A baby's vision changes significantly in the first year of life. Infants initially have a range of vision of only 8 – 12 inches and no depth perception. As a result, they rely primarily on hearing. Vision does not become the dominant sense until babies are around twelve months old. Babies prefer faces to other objects. This preference, along with their limited vision range, means that their sight is initially focused on their caregiver.

12) Which term BEST describes the structure of the text?
   A. chronological
   B. cause-effect
   C. problem-solution
   D. comparison-contrast

THE AUDIENCE

The structure, purpose, main idea, and language of a text all converge on one target: the intended audience. An author makes decisions about every aspect of a piece of writing based on that audience, and readers evaluate the writing through the lens of that audience.

By considering the likely reactions of an intended audience, readers can determine many things: whether they are part of that intended audience; the author's purpose for using specific techniques or devices; the biases of the author and how they appear in the writing; and how the author uses rhetorical strategies. While readers evaluate each of these things separately, identifying and considering the intended audience deepens a reader's understanding of a text and helps highlight details.

> **QUICK REVIEW**
>
> A logical argument includes a claim, a reason that supports the claim, and an assumption the reader makes based on accepted beliefs. All parts of the argument need to make sense to the reader, so authors often consider their audience's beliefs as they make their arguments.

Readers can figure out a text's intended audience by asking a few questions. First, what is the main idea of the passage? Who most likely cares about that idea, benefits from it, or needs to know about it? Answering those questions will help reveal the intended audience. For example, if the main idea of a passage is "signs you need to take your car to the mechanic," the audience is probably car owners who do not have a lot of technical knowledge.

Then the reader considers language. The author tailors language to appeal to the intended audience. Readers can understand the audience based on the type of language used. For example, the figurative language John Steinbeck uses in his novel *The Grapes of Wrath* describes the suffering of Americans who migrated to California to find work during the Great Depression of the 1930s.

Steinbeck spoke directly to the Americans who were discriminating against the migrants. Instead of finding work in the "land of milk and honey," migrants faced poverty and injustice. The metaphor that gives the novel its title is "and in the eyes of the people there is the failure; and in the eyes of the hungry there is a growing wrath. In the souls of the people the grapes of wrath are filling and growing heavy, growing heavy for the vintage." Steinbeck used the image of ripening grapes, familiar to those surrounded by vineyards, to condemn the harsh treatment of impoverished migrants and inspire compassion in his audience.

SAMPLE QUESTION

The social and political discourse of America continues to be permeated with idealism. An idealistic viewpoint asserts that the ideals of freedom, equality, justice, and human dignity are the truths that Americans must continue to aspire to. Idealists argue that truth is what should be, not necessarily what is. In general, they work to improve things and to make them as close to ideal as possible.

13) **Which phrase BEST describes the author's purpose?**
    A. to advocate for freedom, equality, justice, and human rights
    B. to explain what an idealist believes in
    C. to explain what's wrong with social and political discourse in America
    D. to persuade readers to believe in certain truths

Tone and Mood

The **tone** of a passage describes the author's attitude toward the topic. The **mood** is the main feeling or atmosphere in a passage that provokes specific emotions in the reader. The subtle distinction between these two aspects lies in the audience: the mood influences the reader's emotional state in response to the piece, while the tone establishes a relationship between the audience and the author. Does the author want to instruct the audience? Is the author more experienced than the audience? Does the author wish to convey a friendly or equal relationship? In each of these cases, the author uses a different tone to reflect the desired level of communication.

> **TEACHING TIP**
>
> To determine the author's tone, students should examine what overall feeling they are experiencing.

Diction, or word choice, primarily determines mood and tone in a passage. Many readers use only an author's ideas to determine tone. It is better to find specific words from the text and look for patterns in connotation and emotion. By considering categories of words used by the author, the reader can discover the overall emotional atmosphere of a text and the author's attitude toward the subject.

> **HELPFUL HINT**
>
> To determine the connotation of a word, the reader examines whether it conveys a positive or negative association. Adjectives are often used to influence the reader's feelings, as in the phrase "an ambitious attempt to achieve."

Every word has both a literal meaning and a **connotative meaning**. The latter relies on the common emotions, associations, and experiences an audience might associate with that word. The following words are all synonyms: "dog," "puppy," "cur," "mutt," "canine," "pet." Two of these words—"dog" and "canine"—are neutral words, without strong associations or emotions. Two others—"pet" and "puppy"—have positive associations. The last two—"cur" and "mutt"—have negative associations. A passage that uses one pair of these words versus another pair activates the positive or negative reactions of the audience.

> **SAMPLE QUESTIONS**
>
> Alan—
>
> I just wanted to drop you a quick note to let you know I'll be out of the office for the next two weeks. Elizabeth and I are finally taking that trip to France we've been talking about for years. It's a bit of a last-minute decision, but since we had the vacation time available, we figured it was now or never.
>
> Anyway, my team's been briefed on the upcoming meeting, so they should be able to handle the presentation without any hiccups. If you have any questions or concerns, you can direct them to Joanie, who'll be handling my responsibilities while I'm out.

Let me know if you want any special treats. I don't know if you can take chocolate and cheese on the plane, but I'm going to try!

Best regards,

Michael

14) Which word BEST describes the relationship between the author and Alan?
- A. familial
- B. formal
- C. friendly
- D. strained

15) Which phrase BEST captures the author's purpose?
- A. to ask Alan if he wants any special treats from France
- B. to brag to Alan about his upcoming vacation
- C. to inform Alan that he will be out of the office
- D. to help Alan prepare for the upcoming meeting

Meaning of Words and Phrases

Some questions on the exam may ask about the definitions or intended meanings of words within passages. Even if some of these words are new, there are tricks readers can use to figure out what they mean.

Context Clues

Vocabulary-in-context questions ask about the meaning of specific words in the passage. The questions will ask which answer choice is most similar in meaning to the specified word, or which answer choice could be substituted for that word in the passage.

The passage itself can help clarify the meaning of unfamiliar words. Often, identifying the tone or main idea of the passage can help eliminate answer choices. For example, if the tone of the passage is generally positive, try eliminating the answer choices with a negative connotation. Or, if the passage is about a particular occupation, rule out words unrelated to that topic.

Passages may also provide specific **context clues** that can help determine the meaning of a word. One type of context clue is a **definition**, or **description**, **clue**. These are also known as **restatement clues**. The definition is often set apart from the rest of the sentence by a comma, parentheses, or a colon.

Sometimes authors use a difficult word, then include "that is" or "which is" to signal that they are giving a definition. An author also may use a synonym or restate the idea in more familiar words:

> Teachers often prefer teaching students with intrinsic motivation; these students have an internal desire to learn.

The meaning of "intrinsic" is restated as "internal."

Similarly, authors may include an **example clue**, using an example phrase that clarifies the meaning of the word:

> Carly found that yoga was efficacious for the cramping in her leg; the morning after yoga practice, her leg pain was gone.

"Efficacious," which means "effective," is explained with an example showing that yoga resolved the cramping in Carly's leg.

Another commonly used context clue is the **contrast**, or **antonym**, **clue**. In this case, authors indicate that the unfamiliar word is the opposite of a familiar word:

> In contrast to intrinsic motivation, extrinsic motivation is contingent on teachers offering rewards that are appealing.

The phrase "in contrast" tells the reader that "extrinsic" is the opposite of "intrinsic."

Positive/negative clues indicate whether a word has a positive or negative meaning:

> The film was lauded by critics as stunning and was nominated for several awards.

The positive descriptions "stunning" and "nominated for several awards" suggest that "lauded" has a positive meaning.

SAMPLE QUESTIONS

16) Based on context clues, which word is closest in meaning to "incentivize" as used in the following sentence?

    One challenge of teaching is finding ways to incentivize, or to motivate, learning.

    A. encourage
    B. determine
    C. challenge
    D. improve

17) Based on context clues, which word is closest in meaning to "apprehensive" as used in the following sentence?

    If an extrinsic reward is extremely desirable, a student may become so apprehensive he or she cannot focus. The student may experience such intense pressure to perform that the reward undermines its intent.

A. uncertain
B. distracted
C. anxious
D. forgetful

WORD STRUCTURE

In addition to the context of a sentence or passage, an unfamiliar word itself can give the reader clues about its meaning. Each word has separate pieces that determine meaning. The most familiar of these pieces are word roots, prefixes, and suffixes.

Word roots are the bases from which many words take their form and meaning. The most common word roots are Greek and Latin, and a broad knowledge of these roots can greatly improve a reader's ability to determine the meaning of words in context. The root of a word does not always point to the word's exact meaning, but combined with an understanding of the word's place in a sentence and the context of a passage, it will often be enough to answer a question about meaning or relationships.

Table 3.1. Common Word Roots

Root	Meaning	Examples
alter	other	alternate, alter ego
ambi	both	ambidextrous
ami, amic	love	amiable
amphi	both ends, all sides	amphibian
anthrop	man, human, humanity	misanthrope, anthropologist
apert	open	aperture
aqua	water	aqueduct, aquarium
aud	to hear	audience
auto	self	autobiography
bell	war	belligerent, bellicose
bene	good	benevolent
bio	life	biology
ced	yield, go	secede, intercede
cent	one hundred	century
chron	time	chronological
circum	around	circumference
contra, counter	against	contradict
crac, crat	rule, ruler	autocrat, bureaucrat
crypt	hidden	cryptogram, cryptic

Table 3.1. Common Word Roots (continued)

Root	Meaning	Examples
curr, curs, cours	to run	precursory
dict	to say	dictator, dictation
dyna	power	dynamic
dys	bad, hard, unlucky	dysfunctional
equ	equal, even	equanimity
fac	to make, to do	factory
form	shape	reform, conform
fort	strength	fortitude
fract	to break	fracture
grad, gress	step	progression
gram	thing written	epigram
graph	writing	graphic
hetero	different	heterogeneous
homo	same	homogenous
hypo	below, beneath	hypothermia
iso	identical	isometric
ject	throw	projection
logy	study of	biology
luc	light	elucidate
mal	bad	malevolent
meta, met	behind, between	metacognition
meter, metr	measure	thermometer
micro	small	microbe
mis, miso	hate	misanthrope
mit	to send	transmit
mono	one	monologue
morph	form, shape	morphology
mort	death	mortal
multi	many	multiple
phil	love	philanthropist
port	carry	transportation
pseudo	false	pseudonym
psycho	soul, spirit	psychic
rupt	to break	disruption

Root	Meaning	Examples
scope	viewing instrument	microscope
scrib, scribe	to write	inscription
sect, sec	to cut	section
sequ, secu	follow	consecutive
soph	wisdom, knowledge	philosophy
spect	to look	spectator
struct	to build	restructure
tele	far off	telephone
terr	earth	terrestrial
therm	heat	thermal
vent, vene	to come	convene
vert	turn	vertigo
voc	voice, call	vocalize, evocative

In addition to understanding the base of a word, readers should recognize common affixes that change the meaning of words and show their relationships to other words. **Prefixes** are added to the beginning of words and can change their meaning, sometimes to an opposite meaning.

Table 3.2. Common Prefixes

Prefix	Meaning	Examples
a, an	without, not	anachronism, anhydrous
ab, abs, a	apart, away from	abscission, abnormal
ad	toward	adhere
agere	act	agent
amphi, ambi	round, both sides	ambivalent
ante	before	antedate, anterior
anti	against	antipathy
archos	leader, first, chief	oligarchy
bene	well, favorable	benevolent, beneficent
bi	two	binary, bivalve
caco	bad	cacophony
circum	around	circumnavigate
corpus	body	corporeal
credo	belief	credible
demos	people	demographic

Table 3.2. Common Prefixes (continued)

Prefix	Meaning	Examples
di	two, double	dimorphism, diatomic
dia	across, through	dialectic
dis	not, apart	disenfranchise
dyna	be able	dynamo, dynasty
ego	I, self	egomaniac, egocentric
epi	upon, over	epigram, epiphyte
ex	out	extraneous, extemporaneous
geo	earth	geocentric, geomancy
ideo	idea	ideology, ideation
ig, im	not	ignoble, immoral
in	in	induction, indigenous
inter	between	interstellar
lexis	word	lexicography
liber	free, book	liberal
locus	place	locality
macro	large	macrophage
micro	small	micron
mono	one, single	monocle, monovalent
mortis	death	moribund
olig	few	oligarchy
peri	around	peripatetic, perineum
poly	many	polygamy
pre	before	prescient
solus	alone	solitary
subter	under, secret	subterfuge
un	not	unsafe
utilis	useful	utilitarian

Suffixes are added to the end of words. They generally point out a word's relationship to other words in a sentence. Suffixes might change a part of speech or indicate if a word is plural or related to a plural.

Table 3.3. Common Suffixes

Suffix	Meaning	Examples
able, ible	able, capable	visible
age	act of, state of, result of	wreckage
al	relating to	gradual
algia	pain	myalgia
an, ian	native of, relating to	riparian
ance, ancy	action, process, state	defiance
ary, ery, ory	relating to, quality, place	aviary
cian	processing a specific skill or art	physician
cule, ling	very small	sapling, animalcule
cy	action, function	normalcy
dom	quality, realm	wisdom
ee	one who receives the action	nominee
en	made of, to make	silken
ence, ency	action, state of, quality	urgency
er, or	one who, that which	professor
escent	in the process of	adolescent, senescence
esis, osis	action, process, condition	genesis, neurosis
et, ette	small one, group	baronet, lorgnette
fic	making, causing	specific
ful	full of	frightful
hood	order, condition, quality	adulthood
ice	condition, state, quality	malice
id, ide	connected with, belonging to	bromide
ile	relating to, suited for, capable of	puerile, juvenile
ine	nature of	feminine
ion, sion, tion	act, result, state of	contagion
ish	origin, nature, resembling	impish
ism	system, manner, condition, characteristic	capitalism
ist	one who, that which	artist, flautist
ite	nature of, quality of, mineral product	graphite
ity, ty	state of, quality	captivity

Table 3.3. Common Suffixes (continued)

Suffix	Meaning	Examples
ive	causing, making	exhaustive
ize, ise	make	idolize, bowdlerize
ment	act of, state of, result	containment
nomy	law	autonomy, taxonomy
oid	resembling	asteroid, anthropoid
some	like, apt, tending to	gruesome
strat	cover	strata
tude	state of, condition of	aptitude
um	forms single nouns	spectrum
ure	state of, act, process, rank	rupture, rapture
ward	in the direction of	backward
y	inclined to, tend to	faulty

SAMPLE QUESTIONS

In December of 1945, Germany launched its last major offensive campaign of World War II, pushing through the dense forests of the Ardennes region of Belgium, France, and Luxembourg. The attack, designed to block the Allies from the Belgian port of Antwerp and to split their lines, caught the Allied forces by surprise. Due to troop positioning, the Americans bore the brunt of the attack, incurring 100,000 deaths, the highest number of casualties of any battle during the war. However, after a month of grueling fighting in the bitter cold, a lack of fuel and a masterful American military strategy resulted in an Allied victory that sealed Germany's fate.

18) In the last sentence, the word "grueling" MOST nearly means
    A. exhausting.
    B. secretive.
    C. costly.
    D. intermittent.

The Bastille, Paris's famous historic prison, was originally built in 1370 as a fortification, called a *bastide* in Old French, to protect the city from English invasion during the Hundred Years' War. It rose 100 feet into the air, had eight towers, and was surrounded by a moat more than eighty feet wide. In the seventeenth century, the government converted the fortress into an elite prison for upper-class felons, political disruptors, and spies. Residents of the Bastille arrived by direct order of the king and usually were left there to languish without a trial.

19) In the first sentence, the word "fortification" MOST nearly means
   A. royal castle.
   B. national symbol.
   C. seat of government.
   D. defensive structure.

FIGURATIVE LANGUAGE

A figure of speech is a word or phrase with a meaning separate from its literal meaning. Figurative language suggests meaning by pointing to something else. When Shakespeare says, "All the world's a stage, / And all the men and women merely players," he is speaking of the world as if it were a stage. Since the world is not literally a stage, the reader has to ask how the world is a stage and what Shakespeare is implying about the world.

Figurative language extends the meaning of words by giving readers a new way to view a subject. Thinking of the world as a stage on which people are performing is a new way of thinking about life. After reading Shakespeare's metaphor, people may reflect on how often they play a role or act a part. They may wonder when their behavior is genuine, whether they are too worried about others evaluating their performance, and so on. Figurative language—such as metaphors and similes—generates thought after thought. With just a few words, it engages the reader's imagination and adds emphasis to different aspects of the text's subject.

> **HELPFUL HINT**
>
> Aristotle claimed that "the greatest thing by far is to have a command of metaphor. This alone cannot be imparted by another; it is the mark of genius, for to make good metaphors implies an eye for resemblances." The resemblance between two unlike things enables understanding of the ideas suggested by metaphoric language.

A **metaphor** is a figure of speech that expresses an unfamiliar *topic* in terms of a familiar *vehicle*. The familiar vehicle helps the reader understand an unfamiliar topic. Readers reflect on the similarities between the topic and the vehicle and form a new idea about the topic. For example, if a person refers to an issue as "the elephant in the room," the topic is the issue, and "the elephant in the room" is the vehicle. In this example, the vehicle shows that the issue is undeniable or overwhelming.

In **personification**, an object is anthropomorphized—receives a human attribute. In the sentence "The earth swallowed him whole," "earth" is personified: it carries out a human action. Personification may also represent an abstract quality. For instance, a timid individual may be the "personification of cowardice."

A **simile** directly points to similarities between two things. The author uses a familiar vehicle to express an idea about the topic. For example, in his poem "The Rime of the Ancient Mariner," Samuel Taylor Coleridge describes his ship as "Idle as a painted ship upon a painted ocean." Since most readers have seen a painting of a ship, Coleridge uses this knowledge to convey that the ship was completely motionless. Like a simile, an **analogy** is a correspondence between two things; it shows a partial similarity.

SAMPLE QUESTION

Alfie closed his eyes and took several deep breaths. He was trying to ignore the sounds of the crowd, but even he had to admit that it was hard not to notice the tension in the stadium. He could feel 50,000 sets of eyes burning through his skin—this crowd expected perfection from him. He took another breath and opened his eyes, setting his sights on the soccer ball resting peacefully in the grass. One shot, just one last shot, between his team and the championship. He didn't look up at the goalie, who was jumping nervously on the goal line just a few yards away. Afterward, he would swear he didn't remember anything between the referee's whistle and the thunderous roar of the crowd.

20) Which sentence BEST describes the meaning of the phrase "He could feel 50,000 sets of eyes burning through his skin"?
   A. The 50,000 people in the stadium were trying to hurt Alfie.
   B. Alfie felt uncomfortable and exposed in front of so many people.
   C. Alfie felt immense pressure from the 50,000 people watching him.
   D. The people in the stadium are warning Alfie that the field is on fire.

Comparing Passages

Some of the questions in the FTCE Reading exam ask test takers to compare texts with similar themes or topics. Test takers will have to identify the similarities and differences in main ideas, styles, supporting details, and text structures. Previewing the questions and noting similarities and differences in texts while reading will be helpful.

The following passages discuss cicadas, a common insect in the United States. Readers should keep in mind the following questions:

- What central idea about cicadas is being expressed in the passages?
- How does the tone of Passage A differ from that of Passage B?

SAMPLE QUESTIONS

Passage A
Cicadas are familiar to many Americans due to their buzzing, clicking song. In the eastern part of the United States, during the summer the air echoes with the humming of the cicada, an oval-shaped insect that can reach up to 2.5 inches in length. Cicadas are harmless: they do not sting or bite humans. They emerge from the ground in the summer to mate. Cicadas live underground as juveniles, or nymphs, and shed their skin, or exoskeletons, to take on their adult form. Cicadas are found in Texas, the southeastern United States, the mid-Atlantic, and range

up through New York State and southern New England. They also inhabit the Midwest.

Passage B
The sounds of summer in the eastern United States feature the lazy buzzing of the cicada. Did you know that there are actually two kinds of cicadas? Some breeds emerge every year to hum away through the hot summer days. Others spend thirteen or even seventeen years underground as babies, or nymphs, only coming out into the light after all that time to mate and die! Cicadas may look a little scary, but don't worry: they are not a threat to humans. Even though they can get quite large for insects, growing to up to 2.5 inches, they eat twigs and liquid from plants. Adult cicadas do not eat at all. They only live for a short time to mate.

21) What argument do both sources share about cicadas?
    A. Cicadas live throughout the United States.
    B. The sound of cicadas is familiar to Americans in the eastern United States.
    C. Cicadas are dangerous insects because they are poisonous.
    D. American crops are plagued by cicadas every summer.

22) What is the main difference between the passages?
    A. Passage A discusses the geographic range of cicadas. Passage B discusses what they eat.
    B. Passage A talks about the cicadas that emerge every seventeen years. Passage B does not.
    C. Passage A has a more formal tone, while Passage B has a more informal tone.
    D. Passage A argues that cicadas are important in the environment. Passage B warns of their harm.

Answer Key

1) A. Incorrect. The author lists Custer's family members who died in the battle, but this is not the main idea.
   B. Incorrect. The author states this fact, but it is not the main idea.
   C. Incorrect. The author does not explain why the cavalry was formed.
   D. Correct. The author writes, "the allied tribes…decisively defeated their US foes."

2) A. Incorrect. The author describes Molaison's memory loss, but this is not the main idea of the passage.
   B. Correct. The author writes, "From this, scientists learned that different types of memory are handled by different parts of the brain."
   C. Incorrect. The author does explain the differences in long-term and short-term memory formation, but not until the end of the passage.
   D. Incorrect. Although the author implies that memories of physical skills are processed differently than memories of events, this is not the main idea of the passage.

3) A. Incorrect. This is the last sentence of the passage and summarizes the passage's content.
   B. Correct. This is the first sentence of the passage and introduces the topic: limitations on government provided by the US Constitution.
   C. Incorrect. This is a supporting sentence in the body of the passage. These types of sentences give important details that support the main idea.
   D. Incorrect. This is another supporting sentence with details that support the main idea.

4) **A. Correct.** This is the last sentence of the passage and summarizes the passage's content.
   B. Incorrect. This is the first sentence of the passage and introduces the topic: limitations on government provided by the US Constitution.
   C. Incorrect. This is a supporting sentence found in the body of the passage. These types of sentences give important details that support the main idea of the passage.
   D. Incorrect. This is also a supporting sentence with details that support the main idea.

5) A. Incorrect. The author mentions magnetic and gravitational fields on Saturn, not Titan.
   B. Incorrect. The author writes, "Then it passed through the unexplored region between Saturn itself and its famous rings." The passage does not mention any rings on Titan.

READING SKILLS 69

- **C. Correct.** The author writes, "First…it recorded data on Titan's curious methane lakes, gathering information about potential seasons on the planet-sized moon."
- **D. Incorrect.** The author refers to the rings of Saturn, not of Titan, when stating, "Scientists hope to learn how old the rings are."

6)
- **A. Correct.** A company that profits from private tutoring might be biased in a study on the effects of private tutoring in schools.
- **B. Incorrect.** This type of study would likely strengthen the author's argument by reinforcing the conclusion that private tutoring leads to educational inequality.
- **C. Incorrect.** Statements from local teachers would not weaken the author's argument about educational inequality because they are subjective and would not ensure equal opportunity.
- **D. Incorrect.** The study is not focused on college success.

7)
- **A. Incorrect.** This answer choice provides fact-based instructions, not an opinion.
- **B. Correct.** The writer uses the first person, showing his or her opinion, to recommend a French press as the best way to brew coffee.
- **C. Incorrect.** This answer choice provides fact-based information about the process of brewing coffee.
- **D. Incorrect.** This answer choice provides fact-based instructions, not an opinion.

8)
- **A. Incorrect.** There is not enough detailed evidence to infer the Confederate reaction to the march.
- **B. Correct.** The author describes the level of destruction in detail, suggesting it had a significant negative impact on the Confederacy.
- **C. Incorrect.** The author does not describe any response to the march.
- **D. Incorrect.** The author writes, "Sherman estimated his troops inflicted $100 million in damages."

9)
- **A. Incorrect.** The author provides no evidence that invasive species typically help native species.
- **B. Incorrect.** The author writes that the quagga mussels, an invasive species, harmed native species.
- **C. Incorrect.** The author implies that quagga mussels are thriving.
- **D. Correct.** The author writes that "the reason for the cisco's reemergence is even more unlikely. The cisco have an invasive species, quagga mussels, to thank for their return."

10)
- **A. Incorrect.** The author does not address the impact of the gun on troops.

- B. Incorrect. The author does not offer an opinion on the use of the Gatling gun.
- C. **Correct.** The author explains why the gun was created, how it functions, and how it was first used.
- D. Incorrect. The author does not describe the impact of the Gatling gun on combat fatalities.

11) **A. Correct.** The passage explains how a baby's senses develop and allow him or her to interact with the world.
- B. Incorrect. The passage does not tell a story.
- C. Incorrect. The passage is not intended to change the reader's opinions or behaviors.
- D. Incorrect. The passage provides facts, not descriptions.

12) A. Incorrect. The author does describe the development of certain senses in babies in chronological order.
- B. Incorrect. The author does not focus on a cause-effect relationship.
- C. Incorrect. The author does not introduce a problem and provide a solution.
- **D. Correct.** The author draws a contrast between the way vision and the other senses develop in babies.

13) A. Incorrect. The author mentions these qualities but does not give an opinion on them.
- **B. Correct.** The purpose of the passage is to explain what an idealist believes in. The author does not offer any opinions or try to persuade readers about the importance of certain values.
- C. Incorrect. The author states that social and political discourse are "permeated with idealism" but does not suggest that this is destructive or wrong.
- D. Incorrect. The author provides the reader with information but does not seek to change the reader's opinions or behaviors.

14) A. Incorrect. Though the author mentions some details of his personal life, most of his letter is concerned with work-related matters.
- B. Incorrect. Though the author is primarily concerned with work-related matters, he includes personal details and friendly language.
- **C. Correct.** The author and Alan have a friendly relationship, as evidenced by the author's casual tone and his offer to bring Alan a gift from his vacation.
- D. Incorrect. The author's tone is casual, and he includes details that suggest he is not concerned or stressed about how things will go in his absence.

15) A. Incorrect. The author asks Alan if he wants any special treats, but since this is the last sentence of the letter, it cannot be the main purpose.

	B.	Incorrect. The author's tone is not boastful. He discusses professional matters and offers to bring Alan a gift, showing consideration.
	C.	**Correct.** The author is writing to tell Alan that he will be out of the office. The details about his trip and the meeting support this idea.
	D.	Incorrect. The author mentions the meeting but not how Alan should prepare.
16)	**A.**	**Correct.** The word "incentivize" is defined immediately with the synonym "motivate," or to encourage.
17)	**C.**	**Correct.** The reader can use context clues to determine that the pressure to perform is making the student anxious.
18)	**A.**	**Correct.** The context implies that the fighting was intense and tiring.
19)	**D.**	**Correct.** The author writes that the Bastille was originally built "to protect the city from English invasion during the Hundred Years' War."
20)	A.	Incorrect. Because the crowd "expected perfection from" Alfie, the reader can assume they are on his side. There is no indication that they want to hurt him.
	B.	Incorrect. The author implies that Alfie is nervous about taking the shot but not that he feels uncomfortable or exposed.
	C.	**Correct.** The metaphor implies that Alfie felt pressure from the people watching him to perform well. There is no indication that he is threatened physically.
	D.	Incorrect. The author gives no indication that Alfie is in actual physical danger.
21)	A.	Incorrect. Both passages state that cicadas inhabit the eastern United States. Passage A is more specific, stating, "Cicadas are found in Texas, the southeastern United States, the mid-Atlantic, and range up through New York State and southern New England. They also inhabit the Midwest."
	B.	**Correct.** Both passages mention the song of cicadas throughout the eastern United States. Passage A states, "In the eastern part of the United States, during the summer the air echoes with the humming of the cicada." According to Passage B, "The sounds of summer in the eastern United States feature the lazy buzzing of the cicada."
	C.	Incorrect. Both passages specifically state that cicadas are not dangerous to humans.
	D.	Incorrect. Passage A mentions that cicadas are "harmless" but not what they eat. Passage B says that cicadas "eat twigs and liquid from plants" and that "[a]dult cicadas do not eat at all."

22) A. Incorrect. Both passages discuss where cicadas live.
    B. Incorrect. The reverse is true.
    C. Correct. Passage A has a more formal tone, and Passage B uses a more informal tone with contractions and direct address: "Did you know that there are actually two kinds of cicadas?... Cicadas may look a little scary, but don't worry…"
    D. Incorrect. Neither passage discusses the impact of cicadas on the environment.

Mathematics

NUMBER SENSE, CONCEPTS, AND OPERATIONS

TYPES OF NUMBERS

Numbers can be classified into various groups based on their properties.

- **Natural numbers** are the numbers used to count objects: 1, 2, 3, 4, …
- **Whole numbers** include all the natural numbers and 0.
- **Integers** include 0, the natural numbers (also called positive numbers), and their opposites, the negative integers (–1, –2, –3, …).
- **Positive numbers** are greater than 0, and **negative numbers** are less than 0. Both positive and negative numbers can be shown on a number line.

Figure 4.1. Number Line

- **Rational numbers** are defined as any number that can be written as a fraction (a part over a whole, such as $\frac{3}{4}$). Rational numbers include all integers and the fractional values between them.

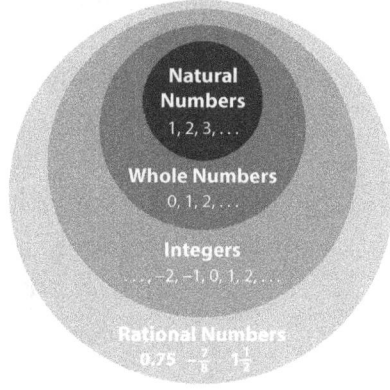

Figure 4.2. Types of Numbers

SAMPLE QUESTION

1) A student claims that "all integers are also whole numbers." Which of the following numbers is a counterexample to the student's claim?

   A. −5
   B. 0
   C. $\frac{2}{3}$
   D. 1

BASIC OPERATIONS

The four basic arithmetic operations are addition, subtraction, multiplication, and division.

Add (+) to combine two quantities. The quantities being added are called the **addends**. **Subtract** (−) to find the difference of two quantities. Subtraction is the opposite of addition.

> **HELPFUL HINT**
>
> The absolute value of a number is the number without a sign.

- If the numbers have the same sign, add their absolute values and give the answer the same sign.

   −2 + (−7) = −9

- If the numbers have different signs, subtract their absolute values. Then give the answer the sign of the number with the largest absolute value.

   4 + (−9) = −5

- To subtract two numbers, change the sign of the second number and add.

   6 − 11 = 6 + (−11) = −5
   12 − (−10) = 12 + 10 = 22

Addition can also be visualized on a number line. Start with the first addend, then move to the right or left depending on the sign of the second addend.

Multiply (×) to add a quantity multiple times (e.g., 6 × 3 = 6 + 6 + 6 = 18). The numbers being multiplied together are called **factors**. **Divide** (÷) to find out how many times one quantity goes into another. Division is the opposite of multiplication.

> **HELPFUL HINT**
>
> The **remainder** is what is left over when one number does not divide evenly into another. For example, when 13 is divided by 4 (13 ÷ 4 or $\frac{13}{4}$), there is a remainder of 1.

- If the signs are the same, make the answer positive.

   −3 × −4 = 12

▶ If the signs are different, make the answer negative.

$-30 \div 10 = -3$

Figure 4.3. Adding Positive and Negative Numbers

SAMPLE QUESTIONS

2) The temperature on a cold day in January was −3°F. When the sun went down, the temperature fell 5 degrees. What was the temperature after the sun went down?

   A. −15°F
   B. −8°F
   C. 0°F
   D. 2°F

3) A case of pencils contains 24 boxes. Each box contains 110 pencils. How many pencils are in the case?

   A. 86
   B. 134
   C. 2640
   D. 5280

EXPONENTS AND RADICALS

Exponential expressions, such as 5^3, contain a base and an exponent. The **exponent** indicates how many times to use the **base** as a factor. In the expression 5^3, 5 is the base, and 3 is the exponent. The value of 5^3 is found by multiplying 5 by itself 3 times:

$$5^3 = 5 \times 5 \times 5 = 125$$

Finding the **root** of a number is the inverse of raising a number to a power. In other words, the root is the number of times a value should be multiplied by itself to reach a given value. Roots are named for the power on the base:

▶ 5 is the **square root** of 25, because $5^2 = 25$

- 5 is the **cube root** of 125, because $5^3 = 125$
- 5 is the **fourth root** of 625, because $5^4 = 625$

The symbol for finding the root of a number is the radical: $\sqrt{\square}$. By itself, the radical indicates a square root: $\sqrt{36} = 6$ because $6^2 = 36$. Other numbers can be included in front of the radical to indicate different roots: $\sqrt[4]{1296} = 6$ because $6^4 = 1296$.

SAMPLE QUESTIONS

4) Which of the following is equivalent to 64?

    A. 2^3

    B. 2^4

    C. 4^3

    D. 4^4

5) Which of the following is equivalent to $\sqrt{100}$?

    A. 5

    B. 10

    C. 25

    D. 1000

ORDER OF OPERATIONS

The **order of operations** is a set of rules for simplifying expressions that include more than one operation. The rules describe the order in which operations should be performed:

1. **Parentheses**—Perform operations within parentheses or other grouping symbols, such as brackets.
2. **Exponents**—Simplify exponential expressions.
3. **Multiplication and division**—Work multiplication and division from left to right. Multiplication does not necessarily come before division.
4. **Addition and subtraction**—Work addition and subtraction from left to right. Addition does not necessarily come before subtraction.

The acronym **PEMDAS** is often used to remember the order of operations.

SAMPLE QUESTION

6) Which of the following is equivalent to $7 + 24 \div 8 \times (4 - 6)^2$?

    A. 1

    B. 15.5

    C. 19

    D. 90.25

Properties of Whole Numbers

Every whole number (except 1) is either a prime number or a composite number.

- A **prime number** is a natural number greater than 1 that can be divided evenly only by 1 and itself. For example, 7 is a prime number because it is divisible only by 1 and 7.

- A **composite number** is a natural number greater than 1 that can be evenly divided by at least one other number besides 1 and itself. For example, 6 is a composite number because it can be divided by 1, 2, 3, and 6.

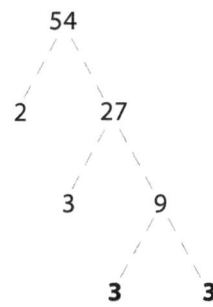

Figure 4.4. Factor Tree

Composite numbers can be broken down into **factors**: the numbers that are multiplied together to produce the composite number. Factors can be found by finding all the sets of multiples that produce the composite number. The example below shows all the factors of 54.

$$54 = 54 \times 1$$
$$54 = 27 \times 2$$
$$54 = 18 \times 3$$
$$54 = 9 \times 6$$

The factors of 54 are 1, 2, 3, 6, 9, 18, 27, and 54.

Figure 4.4 shows how the number 54 can be broken down into prime factors: $54 = 2 \times 3 \times 3 \times 3$.

The **greatest common factor (GCF)** of a set of numbers, also called the **greatest common divisor**, is the greatest number (other than 1) that each number in the set is divisible by without any remainders. The GCF may be one of the numbers; for example, for the numbers 4 and 8, the GCF is 4, since 4 goes into both 4 and 8.

The **least common multiple (LCM)** of a set of numbers is the smallest number that is a multiple of all the numbers in the set. The LCM is often called the **least common denominator (LCD)**, especially when it is used to add and subtract fractions. To find the LCM of numbers, write out all the multiples and look for the smallest number that is in both lists.

> **HELPFUL HINT**
>
> Even numbers are multiples of 2, meaning they have 2 as a factor (2, 4, 6, . . .).
>
> Odd numbers have a remainder when divided by 2.

6: 6, 12, 18, **24**, 30
8: 8, 16, **24**, 32
The least common multiple of 6 and 8 is 24.

> SAMPLE QUESTION

7) In the Venn diagram below, circle A represents all the factors of 12 and circle B represents all the factors of 26. How many numbers are included in the shaded region?

   A. 0
   B. 1
   C. 2
   D. 3

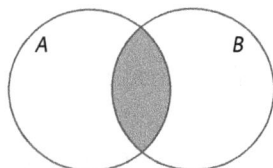

FRACTIONS

A **fraction** represents parts of a whole. The top number of a fraction, called the **numerator**, indicates how many equal-sized parts are present. The bottom number of a fraction, called the **denominator**, indicates how many equal-sized parts make a whole.

Fractions have several forms:

- **proper fraction**: the numerator is less than the denominator
- **improper fraction**: the numerator is greater than or equal to the denominator
- **mixed number**: the combination of a whole number and a fraction

Figure 4.5. Parts of a Fraction

Improper fractions can be converted to mixed numbers by dividing. (The fraction bar is also a division symbol.) The remainder becomes the new numerator.

$$\frac{9}{4} = 2\frac{1}{4}$$

To convert a mixed number to a fraction, multiply the whole number by the denominator of the fraction, and add the numerator. The result becomes the numerator of the improper fraction; the denominator remains the same.

$$1 + \frac{3}{5} = 1\frac{3}{5} \quad \text{mixed number}$$

or

$$\frac{5}{5} + \frac{3}{5} = \frac{8}{5} \quad \text{improper fraction}$$

(↑ proper fraction)

Figure 4.6. Types of Fractions

$$3\frac{2}{5} = \frac{(3 \times 5) + 2}{5} = \frac{17}{5}$$

Adding or subtracting fractions requires a **common denominator**. This value may be the least common denominator. However, the easiest way to find a common denominator is simply to multiply all the denominators together.

> **HELPFUL HINT**
>
> To create **equivalent fractions** (fractions that are equal), multiply the numerator and denominator by the same number.

Multiply each fraction by the value needed to create a common denominator. Once all the denominators are the same, add or subtract the numerators.

$$\frac{3}{10} + \frac{2}{3} = \frac{3}{(3)}\frac{3}{10} + \frac{10}{(10)}\frac{2}{3} = \frac{9}{30} + \frac{20}{30} = \frac{29}{30}$$

$$\frac{3}{5} - \frac{1}{4} = \frac{4}{(4)}\frac{3}{5} - \frac{5}{(5)}\frac{1}{4} = \frac{12}{20} - \frac{5}{20} = \frac{7}{20}$$

A common denominator is not necessary for multiplication or division of fractions. To **multiply fractions**, multiply numerators and multiply denominators. Reduce the product to lowest terms.

$$\frac{5}{6} \times \frac{2}{3} = \frac{5 \times 2}{6 \times 3} = \frac{10}{18} = \frac{5}{9}$$

To **divide fractions**, multiply the first fraction by the reciprocal of the second fraction. To find the **reciprocal** of a fraction, swap the numerator and the denominator.

$$\frac{2}{3} \div \frac{1}{4} = \frac{2}{3} \times \frac{4}{1} = \frac{8}{3}$$

When multiplying and dividing mixed numbers, the mixed numbers must be converted to improper fractions.

$$2\frac{3}{7} \times \frac{1}{2} = \frac{17}{7} \times \frac{1}{2} = \frac{17}{14}$$

SAMPLE QUESTIONS

8) Carla divides her pizza into 8 equal slices and takes 1 piece. If the amount of pizza remaining is written as a fraction, the numerator will be:

   A. 1
   B. 7
   C. 8
   D. 9

9) A student is taking a survey of her classmates for a project. She finds that $\frac{3}{4}$ of students have a favorite book. Of the students who have a favorite book, $\frac{1}{5}$ say that *The Hunger Games* is their favorite book. What fraction of the total class says that *The Hunger Games* is their favorite book?

DECIMALS

Decimal numbers use decimal notation to express fractions with denominators that are powers of ten. Each digit to the right of the decimal point has a place value of tenths, hundredths, thousandths, and so on. For example, the fraction $\frac{319}{1000}$ written in decimal notation would be 0.319.

Table 4.1. Place Value Chart

1,000,000	100,000	10,000	1,000	100	10	1	.	$\frac{1}{10}$	$\frac{1}{100}$
10^6	10^5	10^4	10^3	10^2	10^1	10^0	.	10^{-1}	10^{-2}
millions	hundred thousands	ten thousands	thousands	hundreds	tens	ones	decimal	tenths	hundredths

To convert a decimal number to a fraction, write the digits in the numerator and write the place value of the final digit in the denominator. Reduce to lowest terms, if necessary.

$$0.092 = \frac{92}{1000} = \frac{92 \div 4}{1000 \div 4} = \frac{23}{250}$$

TEST TIP

The Praxis exam includes an on-screen calculator that will allow you to easily add, subtract, multiply, and divide decimal numbers.

To convert a fraction to a decimal, divide the numerator by the denominator.

$$\frac{5}{8} = 5 \div 8 = 0.625$$

Rounding is used to make numbers easier to work with. The process makes numbers less accurate, but the operations and mental math are easier.

To round a number, first identify the digit in the specified place (such as the tenths or hundredths). Then look at the digit one place to the right. If that digit is four or less, keep the digit in the specified place the same. If that digit is five or more, add 1 to the digit in the specified place. All the digits to the right of the specified place become zeros.

Numbers can be rounded to any place value:
- rounded to the hundreds place: 5372 → 5400
- rounded to the tenths place: 11.635 → 11.600

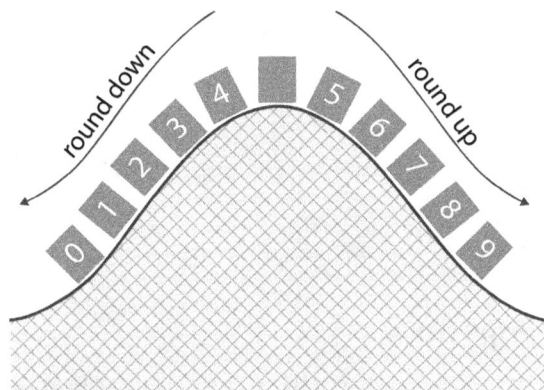

Figure 4.7. Rounding

SAMPLE QUESTIONS

10) Which digit is in the hundredths place when 1.3208 is divided by 5.2?
    A. 0
    B. 2
    C. 4
    D. 5

11) What is 498,235 rounded to the nearest thousands?
    A. 498,000
    B. 498,200
    C. 499,000
    D. 499,200

ORDERING NUMBERS

Some questions on the Math exam may require that numbers be compared or placed in ascending order. Below are some methods that can help make ordering numbers easier.
- For sets with fractions, give all the fractions a common denominator.
- For sets with fractions and decimals, convert all fractions to decimals. (Use the on-screen calculator if needed.)
- Place the numbers on a number line to visualize their relationship.

SAMPLE QUESTION

12) Which of the following numbers would create a list of numbers ordered from least to greatest if inserted in the blank space?

$\frac{1}{2}$, ____, 0.825

A. 1.5
B. 0
C. $\frac{1}{3}$
D. $\frac{4}{5}$

RATIOS AND PROPORTIONS

A **ratio** is a comparison of two quantities. For example, if a class consists of 15 women and 10 men, the ratio of women to men is 15 to 10. This ratio can also be written as 15:10 or $\frac{15}{10}$. Ratios, like fractions, can be reduced. To **reduce** a fraction or ratio, divide each number by the largest factor they share.

$$\frac{25}{15} = \frac{25 \div 5}{15 \div 5} = \frac{5}{3}$$

A **proportion** is a statement that two ratios are equal. For example, proportion $\frac{5}{10} = \frac{7}{14}$ is true because both ratios are equal to $\frac{1}{2}$.

Proportions have a useful quality: their cross products are equal. For the example proportion above:

$$\frac{5}{10} = \frac{7}{14}$$
$$5(14) = 7(10)$$
$$70 = 70$$

> **HELPFUL HINT**
>
> Cross product:
> $\frac{a}{b} = \frac{c}{d} \rightarrow ad = bc$

The fact that the cross products of proportions are equal can be used to solve proportions in which one of the values is missing. (See Algebraic Thinking and the Coordinate Plane and its subsections later in this chapter to learn how to solve simple algebraic equations.)

$$\frac{6}{13} = \frac{x}{39}$$
$$13x = 6(39)$$
$$13x = 234$$
$$x = 18$$

SAMPLE QUESTIONS

13) A company employs 30 people, 12 of whom are men. What is the ratio of women to men working at the company?

_____

14) The dosage for a particular medication is proportional to the weight of the patient. If the dosage for a patient weighing 60 kg is 90 mg, what is the dosage for a patient weighing 80 kg?
    A. 40 mg
    B. 120 mg
    C. 180 mg
    D. 7200 mg

PERCENTAGES

A **percent** (or percentage) means *per hundred* and is expressed with the percent symbol, %. For example, 54% means 54 out of every 100. Percentages are turned into decimals by moving the decimal point two places to the left, so 54% = 0.54. Percentages can be solved by setting up a proportion:

HELPFUL HINT

Key words for percent increase: "markup," "growth," "increased." Key words for percent decrease: "marked down," "sale," "decreased."

$$\frac{\text{part}}{\text{whole}} = \frac{\%}{100}$$

Percent change describes how much a value has increased or decreased. It is found using the formula:

$$\text{percent change} = \frac{\text{new amount} - \text{old amount}}{\text{old amount}} \times 100$$

To find the amount that a value has changed, it's often easier to use the formula given below, where percent change is given as a decimal:

$$\text{amount of change} = \text{original amount} \times \text{percent change}$$

SAMPLE QUESTIONS

15) 16 is 80% of what number?

_____

16) A store owner buys 100 textbooks for $16 per book. If he marks up each book by 8% and sells all the books, what will his profit be?

    A. $128
    B. $160
    C. $168
    D. $1728

Geometry and Measurement

Units

The United States uses **customary units**, sometimes called standard units. Most countries use the **metric system**, which uses a different set of units.

Table 4.1. US Customary Units

Dimension	Customary Units	Metric Units	Converting Between Customary Units	Converting Between Customary and Metric Units
length	inch (in) foot (ft) yard (yd) mile (mi)	meter (m)	12 inches = 1 foot 3 feet = 1 yard 5280 feet = 1 mile	1 in = 2.54 cm 1 ft = 0.3 m 1 yd = 0.914 m 1 mi = 1.61 km
mass	ounce (oz) pound (lb)	gram (g)	16 ounces = 1 pound 2000 pounds = 1 ton	1 oz = 28.35 g 1 lb = 0.454 kg
volume	fluid ounce (fl oz) cup (c) pint (pt) quart (qt) gallon (gal)	liter (L)	8 fluid ounces = 1 cup 2 cups = 1 pint 2 pints = 1 quart 4 quarts = 1 gallon	1 gal = 3.785 L

The metric system also uses a set of prefixes to make it easier to express very large and very small measurements. The prefixes are added to the unit.

$$1000 \text{ meters} = 1 \text{ kilometer}$$
$$1000 \text{ m} = 1 \text{ km}$$

Table 4.2. Metric Prefixes

Prefix	Symbol	Multiplication Factor
tera	T	1,000,000,000,000
giga	G	1,000,000,000

Prefix	Symbol	Multiplication Factor
mega	M	1,000,000
kilo	k	1,000
hecto	h	100
deca	da	10
base unit	--	--
deci	d	0.1
centi	c	0.01
milli	m	0.001
micro	μ	0.0000001
nano	n	0.0000000001
pico	p	0.0000000000001

Units can be converted within the customary system and between the two systems using dimensional analysis. Start with the original unit and multiply by the conversion factor (written as a fraction like $\frac{1000 \text{ m}}{1 \text{ km}}$) to get the new unit. Note that units that appear on the top and bottom cancel out.

$$\frac{120 \text{ in}}{\square} \times \frac{1 \text{ ft}}{12 \text{ in}} = 10 \text{ ft}$$

$$6 \text{ m/s} = \frac{6 \text{ m}}{1 \text{ s}} \times \frac{1 \text{ ft}}{0.3 \text{ m}} = \frac{6 \text{ ft}}{0.3 \text{ s}} = 20 \text{ ft/s}$$

A similar strategy can be used to solve problems that involve a rate, such as meters per second or miles per hour. These problems will ask for quantities like distance or time. Place the standalone value on the left, and multiply by the rate.

How long will it take a car traveling 60 miles per hour to travel 300 miles?

$$\frac{300 \text{ miles}}{\square} \times \frac{1 \text{ hour}}{60 \text{ miles}} = 5 \text{ hours}$$

SAMPLE QUESTIONS

17) Which of the following is an appropriate unit for measuring the height of an adult?

   A. kilometer
   B. liter
   C. mile
   D. meter

18) A 10,000-gallon pool is being filled at a rate of x gallons per minute. Which of the following expressions describes the length of time in minutes it will take for the pool to be full?

A. $10{,}000x$

B. $\dfrac{10{,}000}{x}$

C. $10{,}000 + x$

D. $\dfrac{10{,}000 + x}{x}$

LINES AND ANGLES

Geometric figures are shapes composed of points, lines, or planes. A **point** is simply a location in space; it does not have any dimensional properties such as length, area, or volume. Points are written as a single capital letter, such as A or Q.

A collection of points that extends infinitely in both directions is a *line*, and one that extends infinitely in only one direction is a *ray*. A section of a line with a beginning and end is a *line segment*. A line segment is described by the beginning and end point, such as AQ. Lines, rays, and line segments are examples of **one-dimensional objects** because they can only be measured in one dimension (length).

> **HELPFUL HINT**
>
> Two lines that form right angles are **perpendicular**. Lines that do not intersect are described as **parallel**.

Lines, rays, and line segments can intersect to create angles, which are measured in degrees or radians. Angles are classified based on the number of degrees they contain.

- Angles between 0 and 90 degrees are **acute**.
- Angles between 90 and 180 degrees are **obtuse**.

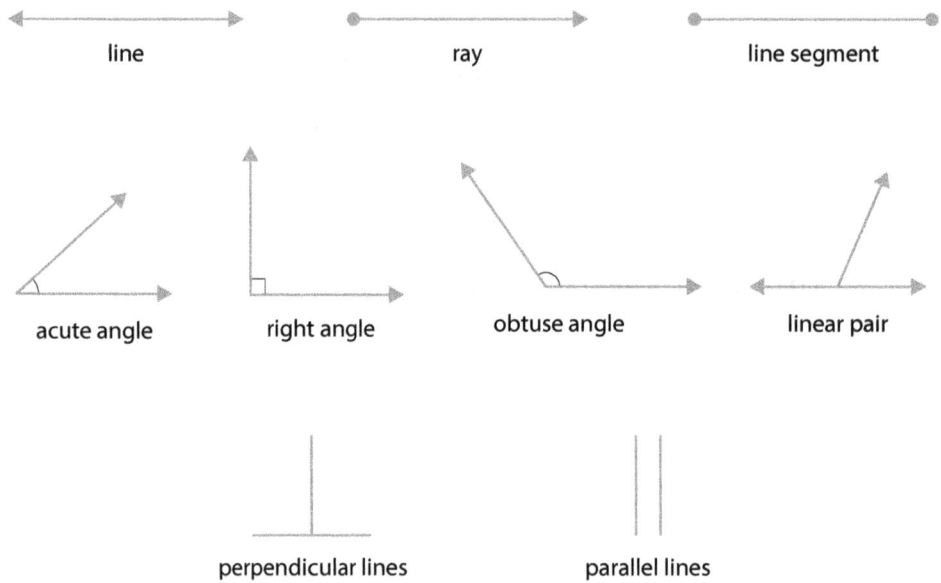

Figure 4.8. Lines and Angles

- An angle of exactly 90 degrees is a **right angle**.

Two angles with measurements that add up to 90 degrees are **complementary**, and two angles with measurements that add up to 180 degrees are **supplementary**. Two adjacent (touching) angles are called a **linear pair**, and they are supplementary.

SAMPLE QUESTION

19) Mrs. Cortez is working with her students on comparing angles. A worksheet includes a picture of the following angle and asks students to draw a larger angle.

Which of the following student answers is correct? Select all correct answers.

[A]   [C]

[B]   [D]

Properties of Two-Dimensional Shapes

Two-dimensional objects can be measured in two dimensions (length and width). A **plane** is a two-dimensional object that extends infinitely in both dimensions. **Polygons** are two-dimensional shapes, such as triangles and squares, that have three or more straight sides. **Regular polygons** are polygons with sides that are all the same length.

A **circle** is the set of all the points in a plane that are the same distance from a fixed point (called the **center**). The distance from the center to any point on the circle is the **radius** of the circle. The **diameter** is the largest measurement across a circle. It passes through the circle's center, extending from one side of the circle to the other. The measure of the diameter is twice the measure of the radius.

> **HELPFUL HINT**
>
> Because all the points on a circle are equidistant from the center, all the circle's radii have the same length.

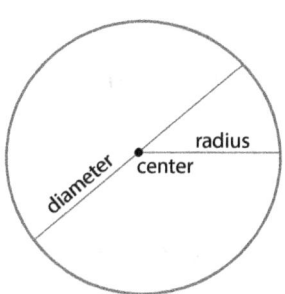

Figure 4.9. Parts of a Circle

Triangles have three sides and three interior angles that always sum to 180°. A **scalene triangle** has no equal sides or angles. An **isosceles triangle** has two equal sides and two equal angles (often called base angles). In an **equilateral triangle**, all three sides are equal as are all three angles. Moreover, because the sum of the angles of a triangle is always 180°, each angle of an equilateral triangle must be 60°.

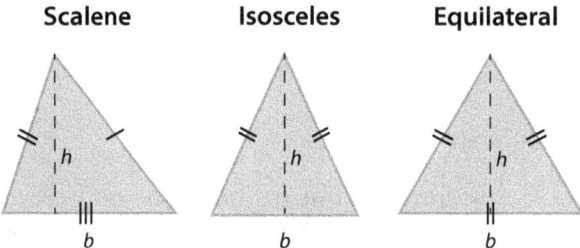

Figure 4.10. Types of Triangles

Quadrilaterals have four sides and four angles. In a **rectangle**, each of the four angles measures 90° and there are two pairs of sides with equal lengths. A square also has four 90° angles, and all four of its sides are an equal length.

Figure 4.11. Quadrilaterals

The size of the surface of a two-dimensional object is its **area**. The distance around a two-dimensional figure is its **perimeter**, which can be found by adding the lengths of all the sides.

Table 4.3. Area and Perimeter of Basic Shapes

Shape	Area	Perimeter	Variables
Triangle	$A = \frac{1}{2}bh$	$P = s^1 + s^2 + s^3$	b = base
			h = height
Square	$A = s^2$	$P = 4s$	s = side
			l = length
Rectangle	$A = l \times w$	$P = 2l + 2w$	w = width
			r = radius
Circle	$A = \pi r^2$	$C = 2\pi r$	C = circumference

SAMPLE QUESTIONS

20) Which of the following expressions describes the area of the triangle below?

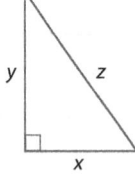

A. $x + y + z$
B. $\frac{xy}{2}$
C. xyz
D. $2xy$

21) The figure below shows a square with four equal cutouts on each corner. What is the area of the resulting shape?

A. 6 mm²
B. 16 mm²
C. 64 mm²
D. 128 mm²

Congruency and Similarity

When discussing shapes in geometry, the term **congruent** is used to mean that two shapes have the same shape and size (but not necessarily the same orientation or location). For example, if the lengths of two lines are equal, the two lines themselves are called congruent. Congruence is written using the symbol ≅. On figures, congruent parts are denoted with hash marks. (See Figure 4.12.)

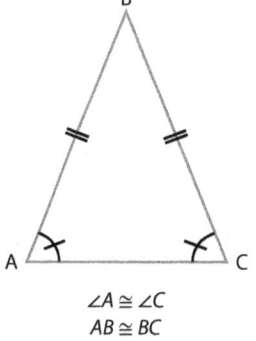

∠A ≅ ∠C
AB ≅ BC

Figure 4.12. Congruent Parts of a Triangle

Shapes that are similar have the same shape but the not the same size, meaning their corresponding angles are the same but their lengths are not. For two shapes to be similar, the ratio of their corresponding sides must be a constant (called the scale factor). Similarity is described using the symbol ~.

ABC ~ DEF

$\frac{AB}{DE} = \frac{BC}{EF} = \frac{AC}{DF}$

Figure 4.13. Similar Triangles

SAMPLE QUESTION

22) The figure below shows similar triangles ABC and DEF.

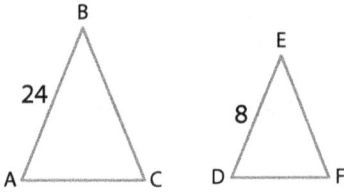

Which of the following statements is true?

A. $DF = \frac{AC}{3}$
B. $DF = AC - 16$
C. $DF = 2AC$
D. $DF = \frac{2}{3} AB$

PROPERTIES OF THREE-DIMENSIONAL SHAPES

Three-dimensional objects, such as cubes, can be measured in three dimensions (length, width, height). Three-dimensional objects are also called **solids**, and the shape of a flattened solid is called a **net**.

The **surface area** (*SA*) of a three-dimensional object can be figured by adding the areas of all the sides. Surface area is measured in square units (e.g., m² or ft²). **Volume** (*V*) is the amount of space that a three-dimensional object takes up. Volume is measured in cubic units (e.g., ft³ or mm³).

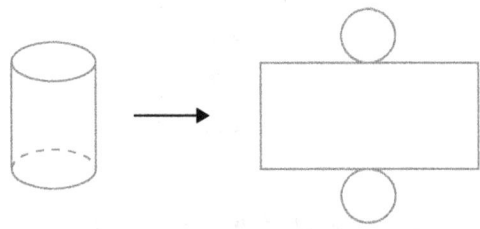

Figure 4.14. Net of a Cylinder

A **rectangular solid** has six rectangular sides. A **cube** is a type of rectangular solid in which all the sides are squares. Every rectangular solid has a width (*w*), a length (*l*), and a height (*h*). Its surface area is the sum of the area of each rectangle, and its volume is found by multiplying the width, length, and height.

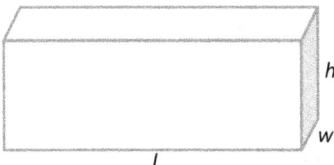

Figure 4.15. Rectangular Solid

$$SA = 2lw + 2hw + 2hl$$
$$V = wlh$$

SAMPLE QUESTION

23) A rectangular tank with a width of 3 meters and a length of 5 meters is filled with 30 cubic meters of water. What will be the height of the water in meters?

_____

ALGEBRAIC THINKING AND THE COORDINATE PLANE

PROPERTIES

The algebraic properties describe basic rules related to addition, subtraction, multiplication, and division. The names of the properties will not be included on the test, but it's important to understand what the properties are and how they are used. Subtraction and division are neither commutative nor associative.

Table 4.4. Algebraic Properties

Property	Explanation	Example
Commutative property of addition	Changing the order of the addends does not change the result.	$4 + 8 = 8 + 4$
Commutative property of multiplication	Changing the order of the factors does not change the result.	$5 \times 9 = 9 \times 5$
Associative property of addition	Changing the grouping of the addends does not change the result.	$(2 + 6) + 4 = 2 + (6 + 4)$
Associative property of multiplication	Changing the grouping of the factors does not change the result.	$(3 \times 5) \times 4 = 3 \times (5 \times 4)$
Distributive property of multiplication over addition	A factor outside parentheses enclosing a sum can be distributed to the terms inside the parentheses.	$7(10 + 3) = 7(10) + 7(3)$

SAMPLE QUESTION

24) Which of the following statements is correct?
    A. $x(y)(z) = x(y) + x(z)$
    B. $x(y + z) = x(y) + x(z)$
    C. $x(y + z) = x(y) + z$
    D. $(y + z)x = yx + zx$

ALGEBRAIC EXPRESSIONS

An **algebraic expression** is a mathematical phrase involving both numbers and **variables**, such as x or a, that represent unknown values. Variables can be multiplied by **coefficients**, which are numbers placed in front of the variable. In the expression $2x + 3$, x is the variable, and 2 is the coefficient. The number 3 is called a constant because its value cannot vary.

A **term** is a collection of coefficients and variables multiplied together, such as $5a$ or $21xy$. The terms of algebraic expressions are separated by plus and minus signs.

Expressions are evaluated by plugging in a given value for the variable. This process has two steps:

1. Substitute—replace the variable with the value assigned to it.
2. Simplify—work out the expression according to the order of operations.

> **What is the value of $3x^2 - 4x + 1$ when $x = 5$?**
> Replace x with 5.
> $3x^2 - 4x + 1$
> $3(5)^2 - 4(5) + 1 = 56$

To add or subtract algebraic expressions, combine like terms. Like terms have the same variable (or no variable) raised to the same power. Note that variables that stand alone have a coefficient of 1.

> **Simplify the expression: $(3x^2 - 4x + 2) - (x^2 + 2x + 5)$**
> Remove the parentheses, distributing –1 to the second expression.
> $(3x^2 - 4x + 2) - (x^2 + 2x + 5)$
> $= 3x^2 - 4x + 2 - x^2 - 2x - 5$
> Combine like terms.
> $= 3x^2 - x^2 - 4x - 2x + 2 - 5$
> $= 2x^2 - 6x - 3$

SAMPLE QUESTION

25) Which of the following is equivalent to $3x(x + 7) + 4x(2x - 6)$ for all values of x?

   A. $7x$
   B. $10x + 22$
   C. $11x^2 - 3x$
   D. $11x^2 - x + 1$

ALGEBRAIC EQUATIONS

An **equation** is a mathematical sentence that contains an equal sign: it states that two expressions are equal to each other. Because the two sides of the equation are equal, the same operation can be performed on both sides of the equation and it will still be true.

Solving an equation means finding the value of the variable that makes the equation true. This value can be found by performing operations so that the variable is alone on one side of the equal sign and a constant is on the other side of the equal sign.

> HELPFUL HINT
>
> To solve a **quadratic equation**, isolate the x^2 term and take the square root of both sides.

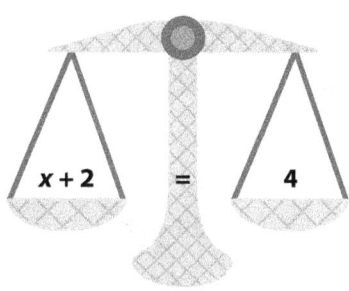

Figure 4.16. Equations

Solve for x: $4x + 5 = 2x - 7$
Subtract $2x$ from both sides.
$4x + 5 = 2x - 7$
$4x - 2x + 5 = 2x - 2x - 7$
$2x + 5 = -7$
Subtract 5 from both sides.
$2x + 5 - 5 = -7 - 5$
$2x = -12$
Divide both sides by 2.
$\frac{2x}{2} = \frac{-12}{2}$
$x = -6$

SAMPLE QUESTIONS

26) If $x + 15 = 4y$, and $y = 6$, what is the value of x?
    A. 6
    B. 7
    C. 8
    D. 9

27) Which of the following statements are valid steps in solving the equation $3x + 9 = 24$? Select **all** correct answers.
   - [A] $12x = 24$
   - [B] $3x = 33$
   - [C] $3x = 15$
   - [D] $x = 2$

INEQUALITIES

An **inequality** shows the relationship between two expressions, much like an equation. However, the equal sign is replaced with an inequality symbol that expresses the following relationships:

> $<$ less than
> $>$ greater than
> $\leq$ less than or equal to
> $\geq$ greater than or equal to

Inequalities are read from left to right. For example, the inequality $x < 8$ would be read as "x is less than 8," meaning x has a value smaller than 8.

Linear inequalities can be solved in the same way as linear equations, with one exception. When multiplying or dividing both sides of an inequality by a negative number, the direction of the inequality sign must reverse—"greater than" becomes "less than" and "less than" becomes "greater than."

> **HELPFUL HINT**
>
> Equations have a finite number of solutions (e.g., $x = 3$).
>
> Inequalities can have an infinite number of solutions, (e.g., $x < 4$).

SAMPLE QUESTION

28) Solve the following inequality for z: $3z + 10 < -z$
   - A. $z \leq 2.5$
   - B. $z = 2.5$
   - C. $z > -2.5$
   - D. $z < -2.5$

LINEAR RELATIONSHIPS

A **linear equation** has two variables, usually x and y. The solution to a linear equation isn't a single value but is instead two values called an **ordered pair**, written as (x, y). For example $(3,3)$ and $(-1,-5)$ are both solutions of the equation $y = 2x - 3$:

> $(3,3)$: Plug in 3 for x and 3 for y.
> $y = 2x - 3$

$$3 = 2(3) - 3$$
$$3 = 3$$

(−1,−5): Plug in −1 for x and −5 for y.
$$y = 2x - 3$$
$$-5 = 2(-1) - 3$$
$$-5 = -5$$

Linear equations have an infinite number of solutions. These solutions can be graphed on the **coordinate plane**, which shows the x-value on the horizontal axis and the y-value on the vertical axis. Plotting all the solutions to a linear equation gives a straight line.

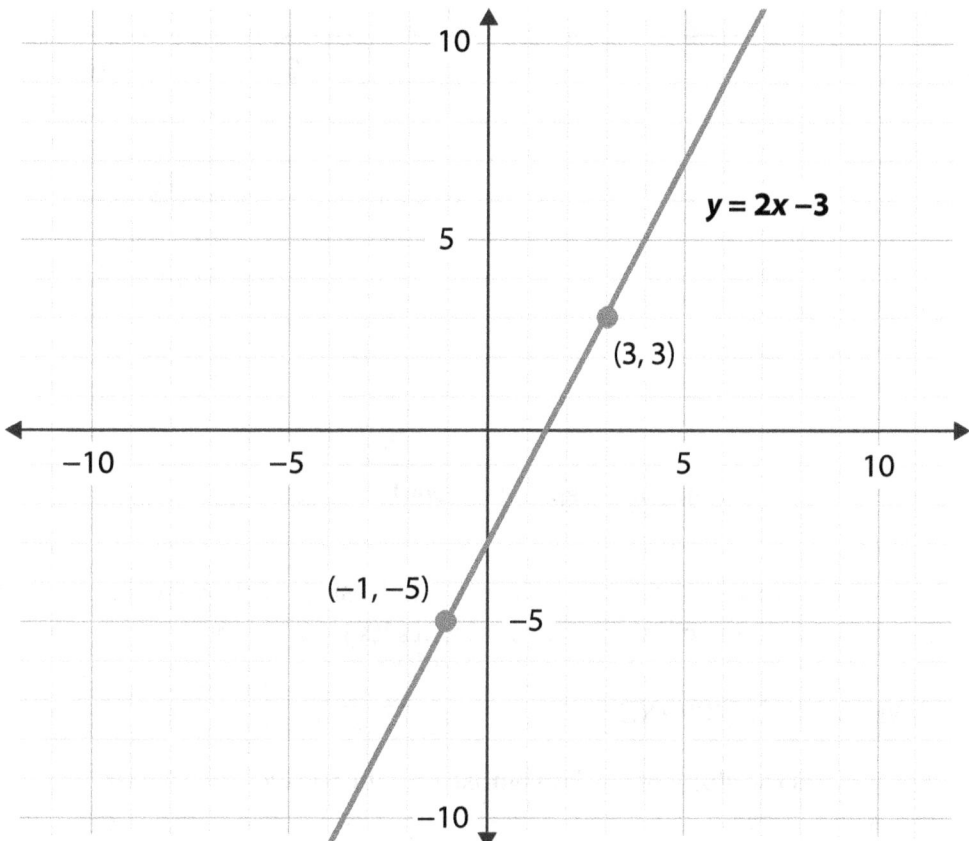

Figure 4.17. Linear Equation

Slope (m) is a number that describes the slant of a line on a coordinate plane. A line with a positive slope rises from left to right; a line with a negative slope falls from left to right. The greater the absolute value of a line's slope, the steeper it is.

To find the slope, choose two points on the graph, and count the difference in the x- and y-values. The slope will be the change in y divided by the change in x: $m = \frac{\text{change in } y}{\text{change in } x}$.

Another useful characteristic of a line is its **y-intercept** (*b*), the point at which the line crosses the *y*-axis. This point will always have the form (0,*b*).

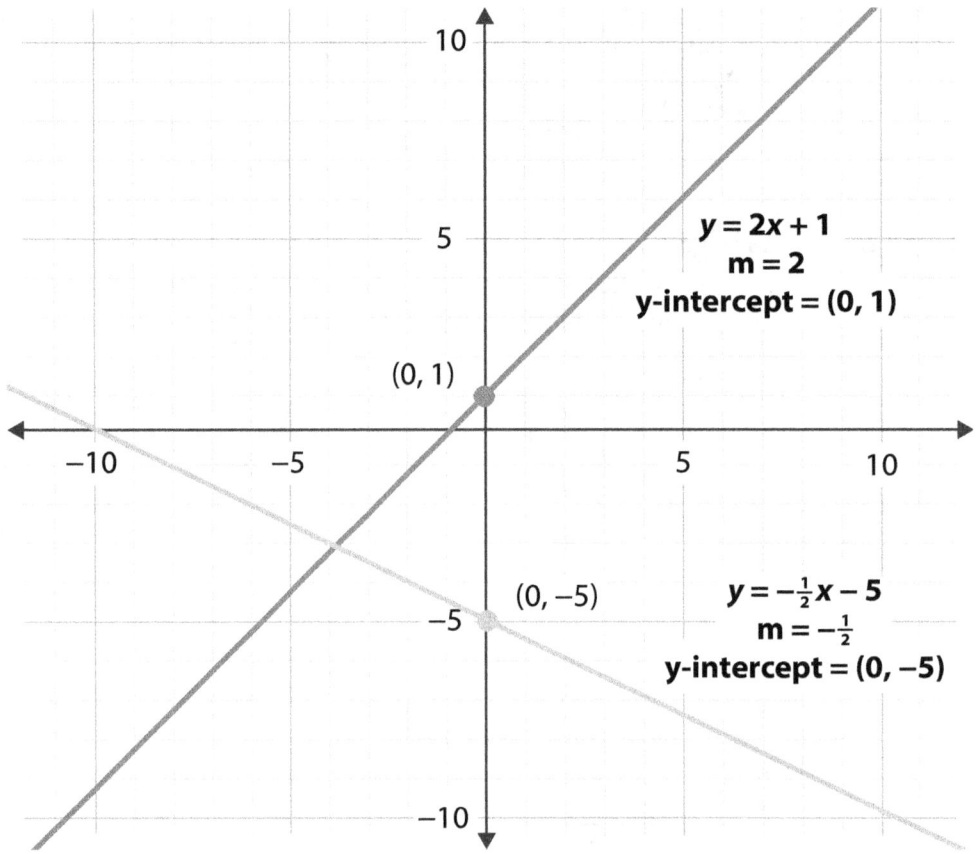

Figure 4.18. Slope and the *y*-Intercept in the Coordinate Plane

A linear equation in the form $y = mx + b$ is in **slope-intercept form** where *m* represents the slope of the line and *b* represents its *y*-intercept.

SAMPLE QUESTIONS

29) What is the slope of the line whose equation is $6x - 2y - 8 = 0$?
    A. -4
    B. $-\frac{2}{3}$
    C. $\frac{1}{4}$
    D. 3
    E. 4

30) The graph below shows the shipping cost (y) for customers purchasing a number of textbooks (x) from a bookstore.

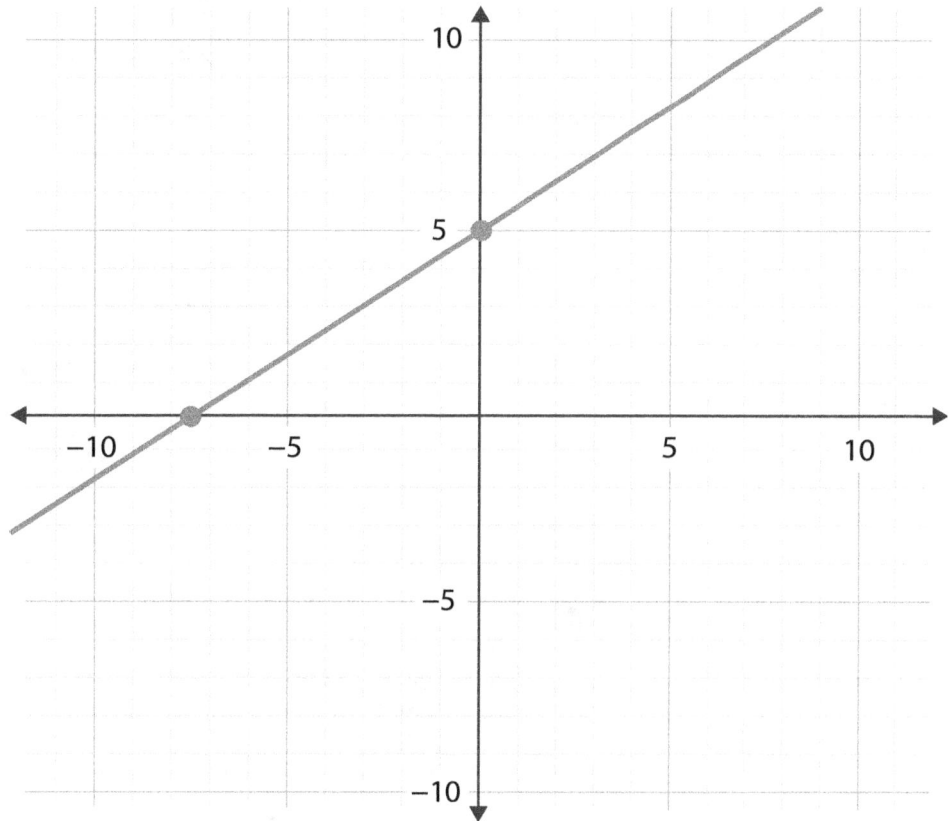

If a customer purchases 100 textbooks, how much will shipping cost?

_____

Word Problems

Mathematic expressions and equations can be used to model real-life situations. Often these situations are presented as **word problems** that can be translated from words into mathematical terms.

When working word problems, start by identifying the known and unknown values. Unknown values can be assigned a variable. Next, write an expression or equation that describes the mathematical relationship between those values. If necessary, the equation can then be solved.

Table 4.5 gives some common phrases and shows how they are translated into mathematical terms.

Table 4.5. Translating Word Problems

Words	Math Translation	Example
equals, is, will be, yields	=	x is the same as y $x = y$
add, increase, added to, sum, combined, more than	+	2 more than x $x + 2$
minus, decreased, less than, subtracted, took away, difference between	−	3 less than x $x - 3$
multiplied by, times, product of	×	the product of x and y $x \times y$
divided by, per, out of	÷	x divided by y $x \div y$

SAMPLE QUESTIONS

31) Joe's Rental Cars charges $35 plus 25 cents per mile to rent a car for one day. If Dan paid $90 to rent a car, how many miles did he drive?

32) Which problems below could be solved with the equation $12x + 15 = 195$? Select all correct answers.

   [A] Marissa has $15. She wants to buy a stereo that costs $195. How much will Marissa need to save each month to be able to buy the stereo in a year?

   [B] Jason has $15 and plans to save $15 per week. How long will it take him to have $195?

   [C] Casey has $15 and plans to save $195 per month. How much money will she have in a year?

   [D] Nate spends $12, and now he has $195. How much money did he have to begin with?

FUNCTIONS

A **function** is a relationship between two quantities (for example x and y) where every value of the independent variable (usually x) gives exactly one value of the dependent variable (usually y). In other words, each input has exactly one output. Graphically this means the graph passes the vertical line test: anywhere a vertical line is drawn on the graph, the line hits the curve at exactly one point.

The notation $f(x)$ is often used when writing a function. The input value is x and the output value is written as $y = f(x)$. To find an output value, plug the input value (x) into the function.

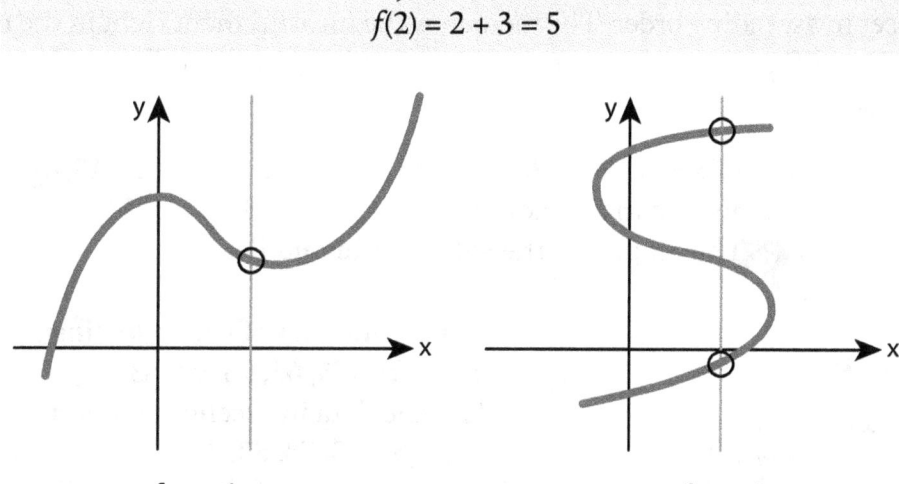

function   not a function

Figure 4.19. Vertical Line Test

SAMPLE QUESTION

33) The table below shows sets of coordinate pairs.

Input	Output
3	6
2	0
5	−4
2	−7
0	13

Is the relationship shown in the table a function?

___

PROBABILITY, STATISTICS, AND DATA INTERPRETATION

MEASURES OF CENTRAL TENDENCY

Measures of central tendency help identify the center, or most typical, value within a data set. There are three such central tendencies that describe the "center" of the data in different ways. The **mean** (μ) is the arithmetic average and is found by dividing the sum of all measurements by the number of measurements.

$$\mu = \frac{x_1 + x_2 + \dots x_N}{N}$$

Find the mean of the following data set: {75, 62, 78, 92, 83, 90}

$$\frac{75 + 62 + 78 + 92 + 83 + 90}{6} = \frac{480}{6} = 80$$

The **median** divides a set into two equal halves. To calculate the median, place the data set in ascending order. The median is the measurement right in the middle of an odd set of measurements or the average of the two middle numbers in an even data set.

> **Find the median of the following data set: {2, 15, 16, 8, 21, 13, 4}**
> Place the data in ascending order: {2, 4, 8, 13, 15, 16, 21}
> The median is the value in the middle: 13

> **HELPFUL HINT**
>
> Adding a constant to each value in a data set will change both the mean and median by that value. Multiplying each value in a set by a constant will also change the mean and median by the same value.

> **Find the median of the following data set: {75, 62, 78, 92, 83, 91}**
> Place the data in ascending order: {62, 75, 78, 83, 91, 92}
> Find the average of the two middle values: (78 + 83)/2 = 80.5

Outliers are values in a data set that are much larger or smaller than the other values in the set. Outliers can skew the mean, making it higher or lower than most of the values. The median is not affected by outliers, so it is a better measure of central tendency when outliers are present.

> **For the set {3, 5, 10, 12, 65}:**
> $$\text{mean} = \frac{3 + 5 + 10 + 12 + 65}{5} = 19$$
> median = 10
> The outlier (65) drags the mean much higher than the median.

The **mode** is simply the measurement that occurs most often. There can be one, several, or no modes in a data set.

> **SAMPLE QUESTION**
>
> 34) A student has an average of 81 on four equally weighted tests she has taken in her statistics class. She wants to determine what grade she must receive on her fifth test so that her mean is 83. What grade must she receive on her fifth test?
>
>   A. 81
>   B. 83
>   C. 89
>   D. 91

MEASURES OF DISPERSION

The values in a data set can be very close together (close to the mean) or very spread out. This is called the **spread** or **dispersion** of the data. There are a few **measures**

of dispersion that quantify the spread within a data set. **Range** is the difference between the largest and smallest data points in a set:

$$R = \text{largest data point} - \text{smallest data point}$$

Notice range depends on only two data points, the two extremes. Sometimes these data points are outliers; regardless, for a large data set, relying on only two data points is not an exact tool. To better understand the data set, calculate **quartiles**, which divide data sets into four equally sized groups. To calculate quartiles:

1. Arrange the data in ascending order.
2. Find the set's median (also called quartile 2 or Q2).
3. Find the median of the lower half of the data, called quartile 1 (Q1).
4. Find the median of the upper half of the data, called quartile 3 (Q3).

The interquartile range (IQR) provides a more reliable range that is not as affected by extremes. IQR is the difference between the third quartile data point and the first quartile data point:

$$IQR = Q_3 - Q_1$$

SAMPLE QUESTION

35) The table below shows the number of customers that came into a restaurant each day of the week. What is the range of the data set?

Day of the Week	Number of Customers
Monday	72
Tuesday	89
Wednesday	125
Thursday	212
Friday	350
Saturday	418
Sunday	262

TYPES OF GRAPHS

Bar graphs present the numbers of an item that exist in different categories. The categories are shown on one axis, and the number of items is shown on the other axis. Bar graphs are usually used to compare amounts easily.

Histograms similarly use bars to compare data, but the independent variable is a continuous variable that has been "binned" or divided into categories. For example, the time of day can be broken down into 8:00 a.m. to 12:00 p.m., 12:00

p.m. to 4:00 p.m., and so on. Usually (but not always), a gap is included between the bars of a bar graph but not a histogram.

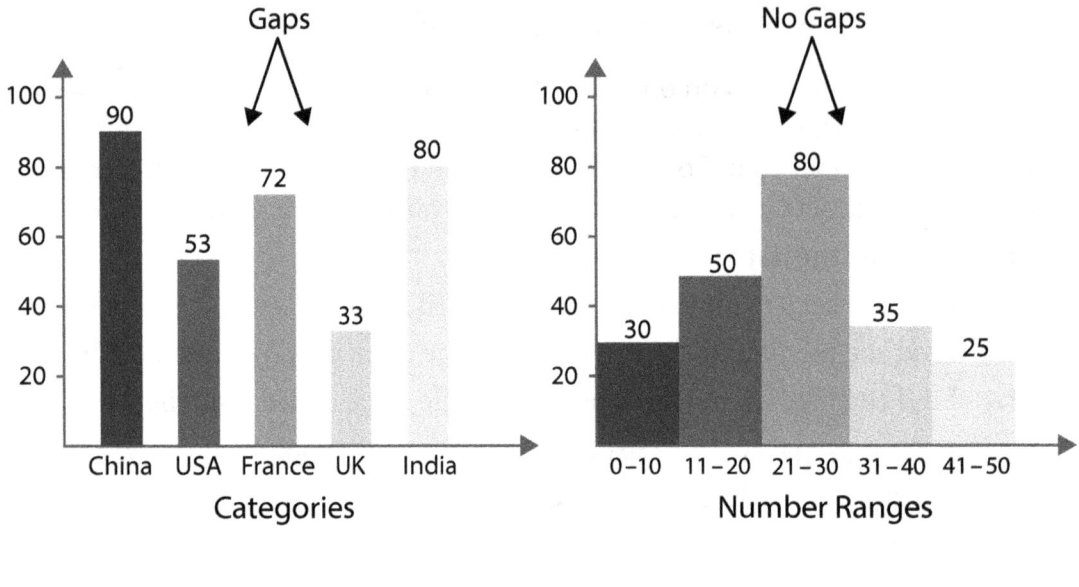

Figure 4.20. Bar Graph versus Histogram

Scatter plots show the relationship between two sets of data by plotting the data as ordered pairs (x, y). One variable is plotted along the horizontal axis, and the second variable is plotted along the vertical axis.

The data in a scatter plot may show a **linear relationship** between the data sets. (See "Linear Relationships" earlier in the chapter for more information on modeling linear relationships algebraically.) There is a **positive correlation** (expressed as a positive slope) if increasing one variable corresponds to an increase in the other variable. A **negative correlation** (expressed as a negative slope) occurs when an increase in one variable corresponds to a decrease in the other. If the scatter plot shows no discernible pattern, then there is no correlation (a zero, mixed, or indiscernible slope).

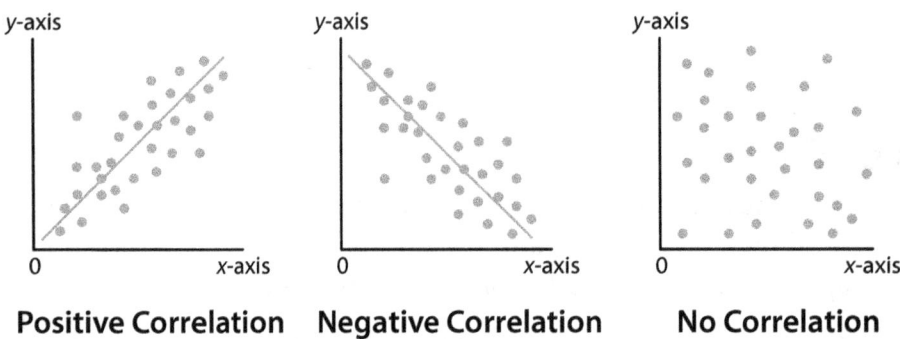

Figure 4.21. Scatter Plots and Correlation

Correlation is a mathematical term that describes two variables that are statistically related (meaning one variable can be used to predict the other). **Causation** means that one variable directly influences another through a known mechanism. Correlation is not the same as causation: knowing two variables are statistically related does not mean one is directly influencing the other.

> **HELPFUL HINT**
>
> In a line graph, each *x*-value corresponds to exactly one *y*-value. A scatter plot may have multiple y-values for one *x*-value.

Line graphs are used to display a relationship between two continuous variables, such as change over time. Line graphs are constructed by graphing each point and connecting each point to the next consecutive point by a line.

Figure 4.22. Line Graph

Pie charts show parts of a whole and are often used with percentages. Together, all the slices of the pie add up to the total number of items, or 100%.

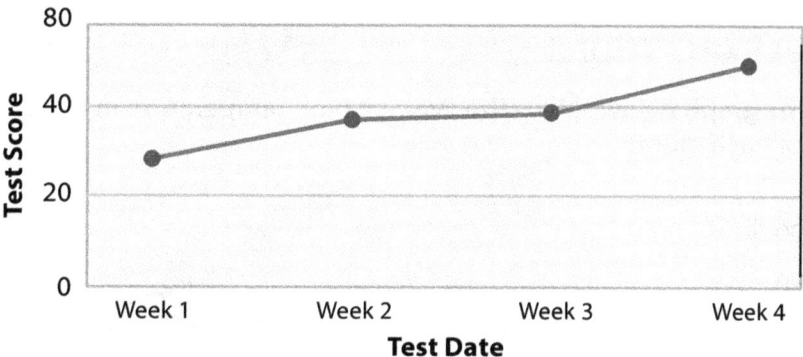

Figure 4.23. Pie Chart

Stem-and-leaf plots are ways of organizing large amounts of data by grouping it into rows. All data points are broken into two parts: a stem and a leaf. For instance, the number 512 might be broken into a stem of 5 and a leaf of 12. All data in the

500 range would appear in the same row (this group of data is a class). The advantage of this display is that it shows general density and shape of the data in a compact display, yet all original data points are preserved and available. It is also easy to find medians and quartiles from this display.

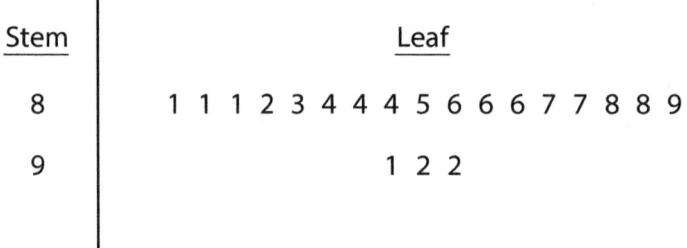

Figure 4.24. Stem and Leaf Plot

SAMPLE QUESTIONS

36) The graph below shows the average high temperature in Houston, Texas, for each month.

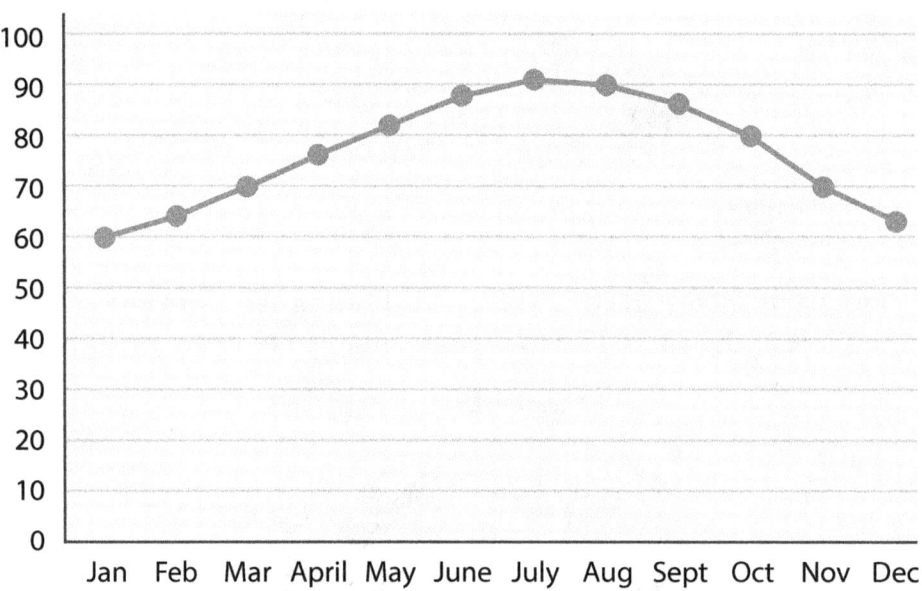

Which of the following is closest to the range for this data set?
A.   5
B.   15
C.   30
D.   60

37) The stem-and-leaf plot below shows students' scores on a recent math test.

9	9, 8, 8, 5, 2, 1
8	8, 8, 8, 4, 2
7	9, 8, 6, 2
6	7, 7, 3
5	5

9|9 = 99

What was the median student score on the test?
A. 65
B. 84
C. 82
D. 88

PROBABILITY

Probability (*P*) is the likelihood of one or a certain number of specific events occurring. The probability of a single event occurring is the number of outcomes in which that event occurs (called **favorable events**) divided by the number of items in the **sample space** (total possible outcomes):

$$P(\text{an event}) = \frac{\text{number of favorable outcomes}}{\text{total number of possible outcomes}}$$

The probability of any event occurring will always be a fraction or decimal between 0 and 1. It may also be expressed as a percent. The probability of an event not occurring is referred to as that event's **complement**. The sum of an event's probability and the probability of that event's complement will always be 1.

If events are **dependent events**, the probability of one occurring changes the probability of the other event occurring. If events are **independent events**, the probability of one occurring does not affect the probability of the other event occurring. Rolling a die multiple times is independent: getting one number does not change the probability of getting any particular number on the next roll.

HELPFUL HINT

An event with 0 (or 0%) probability will never occur, and an event with a probability of 1 (or 100%) is certain to occur.

The probability of two *independent events* occurring is the product of the two events' probabilities:

$$P(A \text{ and } B) = P(A) \times P(B)$$

SAMPLE QUESTION

38) In 2018 in the United States, 3.2 million teachers were employed by public schools, and 0.5 million teachers were employed by private schools. What is the probability that a US teacher selected at random works at a private school?

   A. 5%
   B. 14%
   C. 16%
   D. 72%

Answer Key

1) A.

Integers include both positive and negative numbers, while whole numbers are always positive (except zero). The number −5 is an integer but not a whole number because it is negative.

2) B.

Because the temperature went down, add a negative number (or subtract).

$-3 + -5 = \mathbf{-8°F}$

3) C.

Multiply the number of boxes by the number of pencils in each box to find the total number of pencils.

$24 \times 110 = \mathbf{2640 \text{ pencils}}$

4) C.

$4^3 = 4 \times 4 \times 4 = 64$

5) B.

The square root of 100 is 10.

$10 \times 10 = 100$

6) C.

First, simplify the expression in parentheses.

$7 + 24 \div 8 \times (4 - 6)^2$

$= 7 + 24 \div 8 \times (-2)^2$

Next, simplify the exponential expression.

$7 + 24 \div 8 \times (-2)^2 = 7 + 24 \div 8 \times 4$

Then, multiply and divide, working from left to right.

$7 + 24 \div 8 \times 4 = 7 + 3 \times 4$

$7 + 3 \times 4 = 7 + 12$

Finally, add.

$7 + 12 = \mathbf{19}$

7) C.

Find the factors of 12.

$12 = 12 \times 1$

$12 = 6 \times 2$

$12 = 4 \times 3$

Find the factors of 26.

$26 = 26 \times 1$

$26 = 13 \times 2$

The factors of 12 are **1**, **2**, 3, 4, 6, and 12.

The factors of 26 are **1**, **2**, 13, and 26.

The shaded region will contain the numbers 1 and 2.

8) B.

7 of 8 pizza slices are left after Carla takes 1, so $\frac{7}{8}$ of the pizza remains. **7 is the numerator** of this fraction.

9) $\frac{3}{20}$

Find $\frac{1}{5}$ of $\frac{3}{4}$ by multiplying the fractions:

$\frac{1}{5} \times \frac{3}{4} = \frac{3}{20}$

10) D.

$1.3208 \div 5.2 = 0.2\underline{5}4$

The 5 is in the hundredths place.

11) A.

The 8 is in the thousands place. Because the value to the right of the 8 is less than 5, the 8 remains the same and all values to its right become zero. The result is **498,000**.

12) **D.**

Start by converting the fraction in the list to a decimal.

$\frac{1}{2} = 0.5$

The new list is now all decimals.

0.5, ___, 0.825

Now convert the other fractions to decimals.

$\frac{1}{3} = 0.33...$

$\frac{4}{5} = 0.8$

Find the decimal value that falls within 0.5 and 0.825.

$0.5 < 0.8 < 0.825$

Choose the answer choice with the original fraction.

$\frac{1}{2}, \frac{4}{5}, 0.825$

13) **3:2**

Find the number of women working at the company.

30 − 12 = 18 women

Write the ratio as the number of women over the number of men working at the company.

$\frac{\text{number of women}}{\text{number of men}} = \frac{18}{12}$

Reduce the ratio.

$\frac{18 \div 6}{12 \div 6} = \frac{3}{2}$

The ratio of women to men is $\frac{3}{2}$ or **3:2**.

14) **B.**

Write a proportion using x for the missing value.

$\frac{60 \text{ kg}}{90 \text{ mg}} = \frac{80 \text{ kg}}{x}$

Cross-multiply and solve for x.

$60(x) = 80(90)$

$60x = 7200$

$x = 120$

The proper dosage is **120 mg**.

15) **20**

Set up a proportion and solve.

$\frac{\text{part}}{\text{whole}} = \frac{\%}{100}$

$\frac{16}{x} = \frac{80}{100}$

$16(100) = 80(x)$

$x = 20$

16) **A.**

Use the formula for percent change to find the sales price for each book.

amount of change = original amount × percent change

amount of change = $16 × 0.08 = $1.28

new price = $16 + $1.28 = $17.28

To find the store owner's profit, subtract the amount he paid for the books from the amount he made selling them.

$17.28(100) − $16(100) = **$128**

17) **D.**

Most adults are between 1 and 2 meters tall. A kilometer and a mile are too large for measuring an adult's height. Liters measure volume.

18) **B.**

Use dimensional analysis.

$\frac{10,000 \text{ gal}}{\square} \times \frac{1 \text{ min}}{x \text{ gal}}$

$= \frac{10,000}{x}$ **minutes**

19) A.   Incorrect. This student tried to draw a larger angle by extending the rays farther from the vertex.

B.   Incorrect. This student increased the size of the angle symbol but did not increase the size of the angle.

C. Incorrect. This student drew a smaller angle.
D. **Correct.** This student drew a larger angle.

20) **B.**

The formula for the area of a triangle is $\frac{1}{2}bh$, where b is the base and h is the height. In this triangle, y is the base and x is the height, so the triangle's area is $\frac{1}{2}xy$, or $\frac{xy}{2}$.

21) **D.**

Find the area of the square without the cutouts; each side would be 12 mm long.

12 mm × 12 mm = 144 mm²

Next, find the area of the cutouts.

2 mm × 2 mm = 4 mm²

4 × 4 mm² = 16 mm²

Finally, subtract the total area of the four cutouts from the total area of the square without the cutouts.

144 − 16 = **128 mm²**

22) **A.**

Use the given lengths to find the scale ratio for the two triangles.

$\frac{AB}{DE} = \frac{24}{8} = 3$

The ratio of DF to AC will also be equal to 3 because they are corresponding parts of the two triangles.

$\frac{AC}{DF} = 3$

Solve for DF.

$\mathbf{DF = \frac{AC}{3}}$

23) **2**

Use the formula for the volume of a rectangular solid to solve for the height (h).

$V = wlh$

30 m³ = (3 m)(5 m)(h)

h = **2 meters**

24) **B.**

The expression in choice B applies the distributive property correctly by distributing the factor outside the parentheses to the terms inside the parentheses.

25) **C.**

Apply the distributive property to each term.

$3x(x + 7) = 3x^2 + 21x$

$4x(2x − 6) = 8x^2 − 24x$

Combine like terms.

$(3x^2 + 21x) + (8x^2 − 24x)$

$3x^2 + 8x^2 + 21x − 24x$

= **$11x^2 − 3x$**

26) **D.**

Substitute $y = 6$ into the equation.

$x + 15 = 4y$

$x + 15 = 4(6)$

$x + 15 = 24$

Subtract 15 from both sides to solve for x.

$x + 15 − 15 = 24 − 15$

$\mathbf{x = 9}$

27) **C.**

Subtract 9 from both sides.

$3x + 9 = 24$

$3x + 9 − 9 = 24 − 9$

$3x = 15$

Divide both sides by 3.

$\frac{3x}{3} = \frac{15}{3}$

$\mathbf{x = 5}$

28) **D.**

Isolate z by moving variable terms to one side and constants to the other.

$3z + 10 < -z$

$3z < -z - 10$

$4z < -10$

$z < -2.5$

29) **D.**

Rearrange the equation into slope-intercept form by solving the equation for y.

$6x - 2y - 8 = 0$

$-2y = -6x + 8$

$y = 3x - 4$

The slope is 3, since it is the coefficient of x.

30) **80**

Use the graph to find the equation that models shipping cost. The slope of the line is 3/4 and the y-intercept is 5.

$y = \frac{3}{4}x + 5$

Plug $x = 100$ into the equation to find the shipping cost for 50 textbooks.

$y = \frac{3}{4}(100) + 5 = 75 + 5 = $**$80**

31) **220**

Represent the unknown quantity with a variable.

m = number of miles

Write an equation to represent the facts in the problem. The rental company will multiply the number of miles by 25 cents and add the $35 base charge.

$0.25m + 35 = 90$

Solve the equation.

$0.25m = 55$

$m = 220$

Dan drove 220 miles.

32) **A.**

In choice A, x represents the amount of money Marissa will save each month. It is multiplied by 12 (because there are 12 months in a year) and added to the $15 she had to begin with, for a total of **$195**.

33) **No**

The relationship in the table is not a function because one input value (2) has two different output values (0 and −7).

34) **D.**

Even though the problem does not give the four individual scores, it can be assumed that each test score was 81 (because four scores of 81 would average to 81). To find the score, x, that she needs:

$\frac{4(81) + x}{5} = 83$

$324 + x = 415$

$x = 91$

The student must score a **91** on the last test to have a mean score of 83.

35) **346**

Range is the smallest value subtracted from the largest value.

$418 - 72 = 346$

36) **C.**

The highest temperature is around 90°F, and the lowest temperature is around 60°F. Subtract to find the range.

$90 - 60 = $**30**

37) B.

Count the number of scores: there are 19 total values in the set.

Count from the top or bottom to find the middle (10th) value.

9	9, 8, 8, 5, 2, 1
8	8, 8, 8, **4**, 2
7	9, 8, 6, 2
6	7, 7, 3
5	5

9|9 = 99

38) B.

Use the formula for probability.

$P(\text{an event})$

$= \dfrac{\text{number of favorable outcomes}}{\text{total number of possible outcomes}}$

$= \dfrac{\text{number of private school teachers}}{\text{total number of teachers}}$

$= \dfrac{500{,}000}{3{,}200{,}000 + 500{,}000}$

$= 0.14 =$ **14%**

Practice Test

THE ESSAY

Read the two topics below, and select one as the basis for your essay. READ THE TOPICS VERY CAREFULLY TO ENSURE YOU KNOW WHAT YOU ARE BEING ASKED TO DO.

1

In recent years, catastrophic hurricanes and typhoons around the world have resulted in large-scale destruction and loss of life. However, rapid population growth and the urban development necessary to accommodate the growth have continued in areas vulnerable to storms and flooding, putting millions at risk. Is it possible to allow for economic growth even while keeping people safe?

2

More than ever before, students are subjected to periodic testing. However, many parents and teachers worry that children and teens are encouraged to study for the tests rather than improve their critical thinking and creative skills. Analyze the advantages and disadvantages of standardized testing for students.

In order for your essay to be scored, it must be on only one of these topics, and it must address the entire topic.

In your essay, introduce the subject and then either explain the subject you have chosen or take a position about the subject and support that position. At least two evaluators will read and score your essay. Be sure to define your purpose, provide a clear introduction and thesis statement, organize ideas effectively, provide support for your argument, and adhere to Standard English.

English Language Skills

Read the question, and then choose the most correct answer.

1

Choose the option that corrects an error in the underlined portion. If no error exists, choose "No change is necessary."

The famously high death toll at the end of the Civil War was not exclusively due to battle losses; <u>however,</u> large numbers of soldiers and civilians fell ill and died as a result of living conditions during the war.

- A. in addition,
- B. therefore,
- C. consequently,
- D. No change is necessary.

2

Choose the sentence that contains parallel structure and is most concise.

- A. The public defense attorney was able to maintain her optimism despite her dearth of courtroom wins, lack of free time she had, and growing list of clients she was helping.
- B. The public defense attorney was able to maintain her optimism despite her dearth of courtroom wins, lack of free time, and how many clients she was helping.
- C. The public defense attorney was able to maintain her optimism despite her dearth of courtroom wins, lack of free time, and growing list of clients.
- D. The public defense attorney was able to maintain her optimism despite her dearth of courtroom wins, the free time she lacked, and the list of clients she was growing.

3

Choose the sentence in which the modifiers are correctly placed.

- A. Invented in France in the early nineteenth century, the modern form of the instrument was the result of several changes made to the stethoscope, which was introduced in the 1850s.
- B. Invented in France in the early nineteenth century, several changes were made to the stethoscope before the modern form of the instrument was introduced in the 1850s.
- C. It was invented in France in the early nineteenth century, the stethoscope underwent several changes before the modern form of the instrument was introduced in the 1850s.
- D. Invented in France in the early nineteenth century, the stethoscope underwent several changes before the modern form of the instrument was introduced in the 1850s.

4

Choose the option that corrects an error in the underlined portions. If no error exists, choose "No change is necessary."

In 1983, almost twenty years after his death, T.S. Eliot won two Tony Awards for his contributions to the well-loved musical <u>Cats, it was based</u> on a book of his poetry.

A. *Cats*, having been based

B. *Cats*, which was based

C. *Cats*, because it was based

D. No change is necessary.

Read the passage and then answer questions 5 – 8.

(1) For centuries, <u>artists and philosophers have long debated about the relationship between life and art.</u> (2) While some argue that art is an imitation of life, others believe that, just as often, life ends up imitating art. (3) In no other genre is the impact of art on our real lives more visible than in the realm of science fiction. (4) Great minds of science fiction such as Jules Verne, Gene Roddenberry, H.G. Wells, and Stanley Kubrick have introduced ideas that, though fantastical at the time of their inception, eventually became reality. (5) Many of these artists were dead before they ever saw their ideas come to life.

(6) Some of humanity's biggest accomplishments were achieved first in science fiction. (7) Jules Verne wrote about humanity traveling to the moon over a century before it happened. (8) Scientists Robert H. Goddard and Leo Szilard both credit their work—on liquid-fueled rockets and atomic power, respectively—to H.G. Wells and his futuristic novels. (9) Gene Roddenberry, the creator of *Star Trek*, dreamed up replicators long before 3-D printers were invented.

(10) Jules Verne's work, for example, was the inspiration for both the submarine and the modern-day helicopter. (11) H.G. Wells wrote about automatic doors long before they began to turn up in almost every grocery store in America. (12) Roddenberry's *Star Trek* is even credited as the inspiration for the creation of the mobile phone. (13) Kubrick's HAL from *2001: A Space Odyssey* represented voice control at its finest, long before virtual assistants were installed in all the new smartphone models.

5

In context, which revision to sentence 5 (reproduced below) is most needed?
Many of these artists were dead before they ever saw their ideas come to life.

A. delete the sentence

B. change "many" to "most"

C. change "dead" to "deceased"

D. change "saw" to "witnessed"

6

In context, which is the best version of the underlined portion of sentence 1 (reproduced below)?

artists and philosophers have long debated about the relationship between life and art.

- A. artists and philosophers have examined the facts and debated about the relationship between life and art.
- B. artists and philosophers have hemmed, hawed, and debated about the relationship between life and art.
- C. artists and philosophers have debated about the relationship between life and art.
- D. artists and philosophers have hemmed and hawed about the relationship between life and art.

7

Which of the following introductory phrases should be inserted at the beginning of sentence 6 (reproduced below)?

Some of humanity's biggest accomplishments were achieved first in science fiction.

- A. Therefore,
- B. In fact,
- C. However,
- D. In addition,

8

Which of the following means the same as the underlined word in the sentence?

In baseball today, strict regulations have <u>standardized</u> the design of bats; they used to come in a wide range of shapes, sizes, and weights.

- A. clarified
- B. reconciled
- C. normalized
- D. ignored

9

Choose the option that corrects an error in the underlined portion. If no error exists, choose "No change is necessary."

Interstellar travel <u>is expected to be an even bigger challenge then</u> interplanetary exploration.

- A. is expecting to be an even bigger challenge than
- B. will be expected to be an even bigger challenge then
- C. is expected to be an even bigger challenge than
- D. No change is necessary.

10

Choose the appropriate word or expression to complete the sentence.

The students' _____ behavior drove the teacher to punish the class with extra homework.

- A. confusing
- B. disrespectful
- C. delightful
- D. unlikely

11

Which of the following means the same as the underlined word in the sentence?

Hank was <u>belligerent</u> because he had been robbed.

- A. hostile
- B. sad
- C. worried
- D. loud

12

Choose the option that corrects an error in the underlined portion. If no error exists, choose "No change is necessary."

The <u>painters who are often confused for each other</u> Claude Monet and Édouard Manet shared a few things: they were born only six years apart in Paris, France, and both contributed important early Impressionist works to the artistic canon.

- A. painters whose names are similar and who are sometimes confused as a result
- B. common confused painters
- C. commonly confused painters
- D. No change is necessary.

13

Which of the following means the same as the underlined word in the sentence?

L.L. Zamenhof, an ophthalmologist in the late 1800s, invented a universal language called Esperanto with the goal of <u>advancing</u> international communications and relations.

- A. improving
- B. changing
- C. hastening
- D. celebrating

14

Choose the phrase that provides parallel structure to the sentence.

The field of child development is concerned with _____ of infants and children.

- A. the emotional, the psychological, and biological development
- B. the emotional, psychological, and biological development
- C. the emotional developments, the psychological, and the biological development
- D. emotional, psychological, and the biological development

15

Choose the appropriate word or expression to complete the sentence.

Larry thought his neighbor, Karen, was _____ his morning newspaper, so he reported her to the constable.

- A) pilfering
- B) borrowing
- C) moving
- D) returning

16

Which of the following means the same as the underlined word in the sentence?

Clyde was <u>lucid</u> when he told the paramedics who injured him.

- A. confused
- B. rational
- C. emotional
- D. incomprehensible

17

Choose the phrase that provides parallel structure to the sentence.

Though it is often thought of as an extreme sport, spelunking involves much more than adrenaline: enthusiasts dive into unexplored caves _____ the untouched systems.

- A. to study structures of, take photographs, and create maps of
- B. to study structures of, to take photographs, and create maps of
- C. to study structures of, taking photographs of, and creating maps of
- D. to study structures, take photographs, and create maps of

18

Which of the following means the same as the underlined word in the sentence?

After years of daily observing people in the worst situations of their lives, Austin's behavior became callous.

A. mean
B. insensitive
C. annoyed
D. empathetic

19

Choose the phrase that correctly completes the sentence.

Freediving, which is done without breathing supports like SCUBA gear, is sometimes _____ other underwater activities such as underwater photography, underwater football, underwater hockey, and even underwater target shooting.

A. combined of
B. combined in
C. combined with
D. combined over

20

Choose the option that corrects an error in the underlined portion. If no error exists, choose "No change is necessary."

Though the term "nomad" is often associated with early populations; nomadic cultures continue to exist even today, especially in Europe and Asia.

A. populations nomadic cultures continue to exist
B. populations: nomadic cultures continue to exist
C. populations, nomadic cultures continue to exist
D. No change is necessary.

21

Choose the appropriate word or expression to complete the sentence.

Omari felt _____ in his employment, so he decided to quit his job and go to law school.

A. motivated
B. satisfied
C. apathetic
D. unsure

22

Choose the appropriate word or expression to complete the sentence.

Henry only _____ the problem when he poured water on a grease fire.

A. hurt
B. reduced
C. exacerbated
D. excited

23

Which of the following means the same as the underlined word in the sentence?

Unlike a traditional comic book, a graphic novel is released as one single publication, either in the form of one long story or in the form of an anthology.

A. normal
B. conventional
C. expensive
D. popular

Read the passage and then answer questions 24 – 27.

(1) Becoming president of the United States is a privilege few people will ever get to experience. (2) Since its founding in 1776, many years ago, the country has seen only forty-four presidents in office. (3) Most of them have since left office and have gone on to lead lives of comfort and influence. (4) However, they may never again experience the power or the excitement of their former office, retired presidents continue to enjoy many benefits as a result of their service as president of the United States.

(5) Presidents receive a number of benefits upon retirement, many of which are afforded by the Former Presidents Act of 1958. (6) First, they receive an annual pension payment. (7) The amount of the pension has been reviewed and changed several times, most recently to reflect the salary of a high-level government executive (roughly $200,000 in the 2010s). (8) In addition to their pension, retired presidents and their families are also entitled to ongoing Secret Service protection, which lasts until the death of the president.

24

Which of the following replacements for the underlined phrase in sentence 2 (reproduced below) most strongly communicates the amount of time that has passed since 1776?

Since its founding in 1776, many years ago, the country has seen only forty-four presidents in office.

A. as it is now
B. long before any of our grandparents were born,
C. which no one alive can remember,
D. almost 250 years ago,

25

In context, which of the following replacements for the underlined portion would best begin sentence 4 (reproduced below)?

<u>However,</u> they may never again experience the power or the excitement of their former office, retired presidents continue to enjoy many benefits as a result of their service as president of the United States.

A. Therefore,

B. Consequently,

C. Though

D. Still,

26

Which of the following would NOT be an acceptable way to revise and combine sentences 6 and 7 (reproduced below) at the underlined point?

First, they receive an <u>annual pension payment. The amount of the pension</u> has been reviewed and changed several times, most recently to reflect the salary of a high-level government executive (roughly $200,000 in the 2010s).

A. as it is now

B. annual pension payment, the amount of which

C. annual pension payment; the amount of the pension

D. annual pension payment, the amount of the pension

27

Which of the following would provide the most logical conclusion to the second paragraph?

A. Interestingly, Richard Nixon was the only president ever to relinquish his right to ongoing Secret Service security.

B. These measures ensure that retired presidents, as thanks for their years of demanding service, continue to live lives of safety and security.

C. The Secret Service is a special security task force that is responsible for protecting the president, the vice president, and their families.

D. However, spouses who remarry after the president has left office become ineligible for Secret Service security.

28

Choose the option that corrects an error in the underlined portion. If no error exists, choose "No change is necessary."

Engineers <u>designing</u> seat belts to stop the inertia of traveling bodies by applying an opposing force on the driver and passengers during a collision.

A. were designing

B. are design

C. design

D. No change is necessary.

29

Choose the option that corrects an error in the underlined portion. If no error exists, choose "No change is necessary."

Though professional dental care is <u>relatively wide available</u> in the developed world, the prevalence of cavities is much higher there than in the developing world due to higher rates of sugar consumption.

A. relatively widely available
B. relative widely available
C. relatively wide availability
D. No change is necessary.

30

Which of the following means the same as the underlined word in the sentence?

Cheryl was nervous, but she did not want to <u>hinder</u> her daughter's dream of becoming a firefighter.

A. encourage
B. expedite
C. crush
D. impede

31

Choose the appropriate word or expression to complete the sentence.

One purpose of parent-teacher conferences is to _____ relationships between the school and the families they serve.

A. alleviate
B. create
C. discourage
D. foster

32

Choose the option that corrects an error in the underlined portion. If no error exists, choose "No change is necessary."

Vivariums are controlled, enclosed spaces designed to replicate a particular <u>habitat, and while</u> aquariums and terrariums are fairly common, insectariums (for keeping insects) and penguinariums (for keeping penguins) are less so.

A. habitat: and while
B. habitat; and while
C. habitat, while
D. No change is necessary.

33

Choose the appropriate word or expression to complete the sentence.
It is impossible to _____ the damage resulting from the fire.

A. quantify
B. understand
C. extend
D. improve

34

Which of the following means the same as the underlined word in the sentence?
Julian became <u>frantic</u> when he realized his child was missing.

A. panicked
B. calm
C. frustrated
D. upset

35

Choose the sentence in which the modifiers are clearly placed.

A. Before introducing self-driving vehicles, automated vehicle processes were studied as early as the 1920s.
B. Before introducing self-driving vehicles, as early as the 1920s, automated vehicle processes were studied by researchers.
C. Before introducing self-driving vehicles, researchers began studying automating vehicle processes as early as the 1920s.
D. Researchers were studying self-driving vehicles before introducing them as early as the 1920s.

36

Choose the appropriate word or expression to complete the sentence.
The judge _____ her seat on the bench because she was seriously ill.

A. abdicated
B. maintained
C. abandoned
D. promoted

37

Choose the appropriate word or expression to complete the sentence.
Officers _____ infiltrated the gang in order to gather intelligence.

A. stealthily
B. fraudulently
C. brazenly
D. openly

38

Which of the following means the same as the underlined word in the sentence?

The American Academy of Arts and Sciences includes members whose topics of study span many <u>disciplines</u> such as math, science, arts, humanities, public affairs, and business.

- A. locations
- B. regions
- C. punishments
- D. fields

39

Choose the option that corrects an error in the underlined portion. If no error exists, choose "No change is necessary."

The Cult Awareness Network, created to provide the public <u>with facts and information</u> about groups whose activities were considered cult-like, was disbanded in 1996.

- A. with facts, figures, and information
- B. with information
- C. with facts and detailed information
- D. No change is necessary.

40

Choose the appropriate word or expression to complete the sentence.

After working several days in a row, Rhonda developed a constant, _____ cough she could not get rid of.

- A. mild
- B. intermittent
- C. persistent
- D. bearable

READING

Read the passage or graphic, and then answer the questions that follow.

Use the following passage for questions 1–5.

In recent decades, jazz has been associated with New Orleans and festivals like Mardi Gras, but in the 1920s, jazz was a booming trend whose influence reached into many aspects of American culture. In fact, the years between World War I and the Great Depression were known as the Jazz Age, a term coined by F. Scott Fitzgerald in his famous novel *The Great Gatsby*. Sometimes also called the Roaring Twenties, this time period saw major urban centers experiencing new economic, cultural, and artistic vitality. In the United States, musicians flocked to cities like New York and Chicago, which became famous hubs for jazz musicians. Ella Fitzgerald, for example, moved from Virginia to New York City to begin her much-lauded singing career, and jazz pioneer Louis Armstrong got his big break in Chicago.

Jazz music was played by and for a more expressive and freed populace than the United States had previously seen. Women gained the right to vote and were openly seen drinking and dancing to jazz music. This period marked the emergence of the flapper, a woman determined to make a statement about her new role in society. Jazz music also provided the soundtrack for the explosion of African American art and culture now known as the Harlem Renaissance. In addition to Fitzgerald and Armstrong, numerous musicians, including Duke Ellington, Fats Waller, and Bessie Smith, promoted their distinctive and complex music as an integral part of the emerging African American culture.

1

What is the main idea of the passage?

A. People should associate jazz music with the 1920s, not modern New Orleans.

B. Jazz music played an important role in many cultural movements of the 1920s.

C. Many famous jazz musicians began their careers in New York City and Chicago.

D. African Americans were instrumental in launching jazz into mainstream culture.

2

The passage supports which of the following claims about jazz music?

A. Jazz music was important to minority groups struggling for social equality in the 1920s.

B. Duke Ellington, Fats Waller, and Bessie Smith were the most important jazz musicians of the Harlem Renaissance.

C. Women gained the right to vote with the help of jazz musicians.

D. Duke Ellington, Fats Waller, and Bessie Smith all supported women's right to vote.

3

The primary purpose of the passage is to

A. explain the role jazz musicians played in the Harlem Renaissance.

B. inform the reader about the many important musicians playing jazz in the 1920s.

C. discuss how jazz influenced important cultural movements in the 1920s.

D. provide a history of jazz music in the 20th century.

4

Which of the following is NOT a fact stated in the passage?

A. The years between World War I and the Great Depression were known as the Jazz Age.

B. Ella Fitzgerald and Louis Armstrong both moved to New York City to start their music careers.

C. Women danced to jazz music during the 1920s to make a statement about their role in society.

D. Jazz music was an integral part of the emerging African American culture of the 1920s.

5

Which conclusion about jazz music is supported by the passage?

A. F. Scott Fitzgerald supported jazz musicians in New York and Chicago.

B. Jazz music is no longer as popular as it once was.

C. Both women and African Americans used jazz music as a way of expressing their newfound freedom.

D. Flappers and African American musicians worked together to produce jazz music.

Use the following passage for question 6.

It has now been two decades since the introduction of thermonuclear fusion weapons into the military inventories of the great powers, and more than a decade since the United States, Great Britain, and the Soviet Union ceased to test nuclear weapons in the atmosphere. Today our understanding of the technology of thermonuclear weapons seems highly advanced, but our knowledge of the physical and biological consequences of nuclear war is continuously evolving.

6

The passage is primarily concerned with

A. the impact of thermonuclear weapons on the military.

B. the technology of thermonuclear weapons.

C. atmospheric testing of nuclear weapons.

D. the physical and biological consequences of nuclear war.

Use the following passage for question 7.

> In Greek mythology, two gods, Epimetheus and Prometheus, were given the work of creating living things. Epimetheus gave good powers to the different animals. To the lion he gave strength; to the bird, swiftness; to the fox, sagacity; and so on. Eventually, all of the good gifts had been bestowed, and there was nothing left for humans. As a result, Prometheus returned to heaven and brought down fire, which he gave to humans. With fire, human beings could protect themselves by making weapons. Over time, humans developed civilization.

7

As used in the passage, "bestowed" most nearly means
- A. purchased.
- B. forgotten.
- C. accepted.
- D. given.

Use the following passage for questions 8–10.

> It could be said that the great battle between the North and South we call the Civil War was a battle for individual identity. The states of the South had their own culture, one based on farming, independence, and the rights of both man and state to determine their own paths. Similarly, the North had forged its own identity as a center of centralized commerce and manufacturing. This clash of lifestyles was bound to create tension, and this tension was bound to lead to war. But people who try to sell you this narrative are wrong. The Civil War was not a battle of cultural identities—it was a battle about slavery. All other explanations for the war are either a direct consequence of the South's desire for wealth at the expense of her fellow man or a fanciful invention to cover up this sad portion of our nation's history. And it cannot be denied that this time in our past was very sad indeed.

8

The primary purpose of the passage is to
- A. convince readers that slavery was the main cause of the Civil War.
- B. illustrate the cultural differences between the North and the South before the Civil War.
- C. persuade readers that the North deserved to win the Civil War.
- D. demonstrate that the history of the Civil War is too complicated to be understood clearly.

9

As used in the passage, "fanciful" most nearly means

A. complicated.

B. imaginative.

C. successful.

D. unfortunate.

10

What is the main idea of the passage?

A. The Civil War was the result of cultural differences between the North and South.

B. The Civil War was caused by the South's reliance on slave labor.

C. The North's use of commerce and manufacturing allowed it to win the war.

D. The South's belief in the rights of man and state cost the war.

Use the following passage for question 11.

> After looking at five houses, Robert and I have decided to buy the one on Forest Road. The first two homes we visited didn't have the space we need—the first had only one bathroom, and the second did not have a guest bedroom. The third house, on Pine Street, had enough space inside but didn't have a big enough yard for our three dogs. The fourth house we looked at, on Rice Avenue, was stunning but well above our price range. The last home, on Forest Road, wasn't in the neighborhood we wanted to live in. However, it had the right amount of space for the right price.

11

What is the author's conclusion about the house on Pine Street?

A. The house did not have enough bedrooms.

B. The house did not have a big enough yard.

C. The house was not in the right neighborhood.

D. The house was too expensive.

Use the following passage for question 12.

> For an adult to be unable to swim is criminal negligence: every man, woman, and child should learn. A person who cannot swim is a danger not only to himself but also to the people around him. Children as early as the age of four may acquire the art; no one is too young or too old.

12

Which of the following best captures the author's purpose?

A. to encourage the reader to learn to swim
B. to explain how people who cannot swim are a danger to others
C. to inform the reader that it is never too late to learn to swim
D. to argue that people who cannot swim should be punished

Use the following passage and graph for questions 13 and 14.

As you can see from the graph, my babysitting business has been really successful. The year started with a busy couple of months—several snows combined with a large number of requests for Valentine's Day services boosted our sales quite a bit. The spring months have admittedly been a bit slow, but we're hoping for a big summer once school gets out. Several clients have already put in requests for our services!

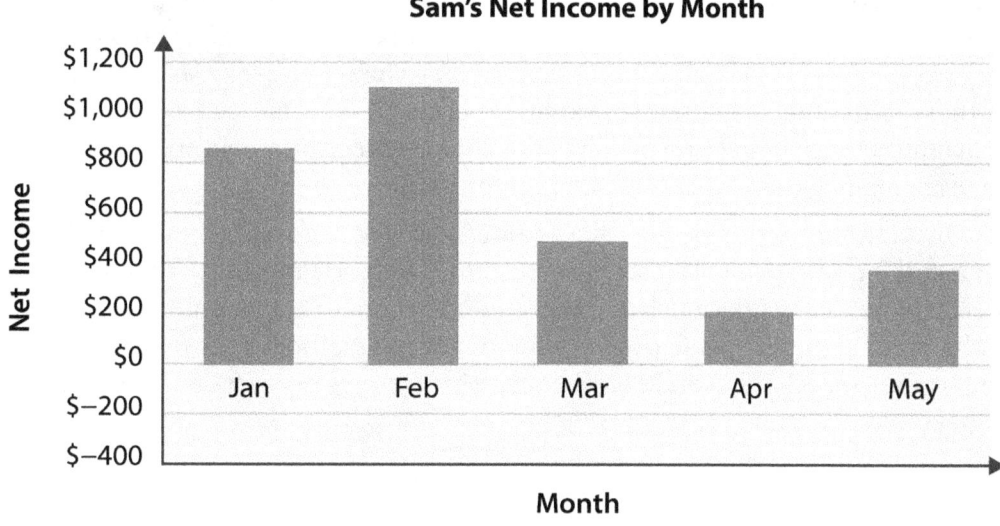

13

Based on the information in the graph, how much more did Sam's Babysitting Service bring in during February than during April?

A. $200
B. $900
C. $1,100
D. $1,300

14

Which of the following best describes the tone of the passage?

A. professional
B. casual
C. concerned
D. neutral

Use the following passage for questions 15–19.

Taking a person's temperature is one of the most basic and common health care tasks. Everyone from nurses to emergency medical technicians to concerned parents should be able to grab a thermometer to take a patient or loved one's temperature. But what's the best way to get an accurate reading? The answer depends on the situation.

The most common way people measure body temperature is orally. A simple digital or disposable thermometer is placed under the tongue for a few minutes, and the task is done. There are many situations, however, when measuring temperature orally isn't an option. For example, when a person can't breathe through the nose, they won't be able to keep their mouth closed long enough to get an accurate reading. In these situations, it's often preferable to place the thermometer in the rectum or armpit. Using the rectum also has the added benefit of providing a much more accurate reading than other locations can provide.

In addition, certain people, like agitated patients or fussy babies, won't be able to sit still long enough for an accurate reading. In these situations, it's best to use a thermometer that works much more quickly, such as one that measures temperature in the ear or at the temporal artery. No matter which method is chosen, however, it's important to check the average temperature for each region, as it can vary by several degrees.

15

Which statement is NOT a fact from the passage?

A. Taking a temperature in the ear or at the temporal artery is more accurate than taking it orally.
B. If an individual cannot breathe through the nose, taking their temperature orally will likely give an inaccurate reading.
C. The standard human body temperature varies depending on whether it's measured in the mouth, rectum, armpit, ear, or temporal artery.
D. The most common way to measure temperature is by placing a thermometer in the mouth.

16

The primary purpose of the passage is to

A. advocate for the use of thermometers that measure temperature in the ear or at the temporal artery.

B. explain the methods available to measure a person's temperature and the situation where each method is appropriate.

C. warn readers that the average temperature of the human body varies by region.

D. discuss how nurses use different types of thermometers depending on the type of patient they are examining.

17

Which of the following is the best summary of this passage?

A. It's important that everyone know the best way to take a person's temperature in any given situation.

B. The most common method of taking a person's temperature—orally—isn't appropriate in some situations.

C. The most accurate way to take a temperature is placing a digital thermometer in the rectum.

D. There are many different ways to take a person's temperature, and which is appropriate will depend on the situation.

18

As used in the passage, "agitated" most nearly means

A. obviously upset.

B. quickly moving.

C. violently ill.

D. slightly dirty.

19

According to the passage, why is it sometimes preferable to take a person's temperature rectally?

A. Rectal readings are more accurate than oral readings.

B. Many people cannot sit still long enough to have their temperatures taken orally.

C. Temperature readings can vary widely between regions of the body.

D. Many people do not have access to quick-acting thermometers.

Use the following passage for question 20.

When the Spanish-American War broke out in 1898, the US Army was small and understaffed. President William McKinley called for 1,250 volunteers, primarily from the Southwest, to serve in the First US Volunteer Cavalry. Eager to fight, the ranks were quickly filled by a diverse group of cowboys, gold prospectors, hunters, gamblers, Native Americans, veterans, police officers, and college students looking for an adventure. The officer corps was composed of veterans of the Civil War and the Indian Wars. With more volunteers than it could accept, the army set high standards: all the recruits had to be skilled on horseback and with guns. Consequently, they became known as the Rough Riders.

20

According to the passage, all the recruits were required to
- A. have previously fought in a war.
- B. be American citizens.
- C. live in the Southwest.
- D. ride a horse well.

Use the following passage for questions 21–26.

Popcorn is often associated with fun and festivities, both in and out of the home. It's eaten in theaters, usually after being salted and smothered in butter, and in homes, fresh from the microwave. But popcorn isn't just for fun—it's also a multimillion-dollar-a-year industry with a long and fascinating history.

While popcorn might seem like a modern invention, its history actually dates back thousands of years, making it one of the oldest snack foods enjoyed around the world. Popcorn is believed by food historians to be one of the earliest uses of cultivated corn. In 1948, Herbert Dick and Earle Smith discovered old popcorn dating back 4,000 years in the New Mexico Bat Cave. For the Aztec Indians who called the caves home, popcorn (or *momochitl*) played an important role in society, both as a food staple and in ceremonies. The Aztecs cooked popcorn by heating sand in a fire; when it was heated, kernels were added and would pop when exposed to the heat of the sand.

The American love affair with popcorn began in 1912, when popcorn was first sold in theaters. The popcorn industry flourished during the Great Depression when it was advertised as a wholesome and economical food. Selling for five to ten cents a bag, it was a luxury that the downtrodden could afford. With the introduction of mobile popcorn machines at the World's Columbian Exposition, popcorn moved from the theater into fairs and parks. Popcorn continued to rule the snack food kingdom until the rise in popularity of home televisions during the 1950s.

The popcorn industry reacted to the decline in sales quickly by introducing pre-popped and unpopped popcorn for home consumption. However, it wasn't until microwave popcorn became commercially available in 1981 that at-home popcorn consumption began to grow exponentially. With the wide availability of microwaves in the United States, popcorn also began popping up in offices and hotel rooms. However, the home still remains the most popular popcorn eating spot: today, 70 percent of the 16 billion quarts of popcorn consumed annually in the United States are eaten at home.

21

The passage supports which of the following claims about popcorn?

A. People ate less popcorn in the 1950s than in previous decades because they went to the movies less.

B. Without mobile popcorn machines, people would not have been able to eat popcorn during the Great Depression.

C. People enjoyed popcorn during the Great Depression because it was a luxury food.

D. During the 1800s, people began abandoning theaters to go to fairs and festivals.

22

As used in the passage, "staple" most nearly means

A. something produced only for special occasions.

B. something produced regularly in large quantities.

C. something produced by cooking.

D. something fastened together securely.

23

Which factor does the author of the passage credit for the growth of the popcorn industry in the United States?

A. the use of popcorn in ancient Aztec ceremonies

B. the growth of the home television industry

C. the marketing of popcorn during the Great Depression

D. the nutritional value of popcorn

24

What is the best summary of this passage?

A. Popcorn is a popular snack food that dates back thousands of years. Its popularity in the United States has been tied to the growth of theaters and the availability of microwaves.

B. Popcorn has been a popular snack food for thousands of years. Archaeologists have found evidence that many ancient cultures used popcorn as a food staple and in ceremonies.

C. Popcorn was first introduced to America in 1912, and its popularity has grown exponentially since then. Today, over 16 billion quarts of popcorn are consumed in the United States annually.

D. Popcorn is a versatile snack food that can be eaten with butter or other toppings. It can also be cooked in a number of different ways, including in microwaves.

25

The primary purpose of the passage is to

A. explain how microwaves affected the popcorn industry.

B. show that popcorn is older than many people realize.

C. illustrate the history of popcorn from ancient cultures to modern times.

D. demonstrate the importance of popcorn in various cultures.

26

Which of the following is NOT a fact stated in the passage?

A. Archaeologists have found popcorn dating back 4,000 years.

B. Popcorn was first sold in theaters in 1912.

C. Consumption of popcorn dropped in 1981 with the growing popularity of home televisions.

D. Seventy percent of the popcorn consumed in the United States is eaten in homes.

Use the following passage for question 27.

The Scream of Nature by Edvard Munch is one of the world's best known and most desirable artworks. While most people think of it as a single painting, the iconic creation actually has four different versions: two paintings and two pastels. In 2012, one of the pastels earned the fourth highest price paid for a painting at auction when it was sold for almost $120 million. The three others are not for sale; the Munch Museum in Oslo holds a painted version and a pastel version, while the National Gallery in Oslo holds the other painting. However, the desire to acquire them has been just as strong: in 1994 the National Gallery's version was stolen, and in 2004 the painting at the Munch Museum was stolen at gunpoint in the middle of the day. Both paintings were eventually recovered.

27

The primary purpose of the passage is to

A. describe the image depicted in *The Scream in Nature*.

B. explain the origin of the painting *The Scream in Nature*.

C. clarify the number of versions of *The Scream in Nature* that exist.

D. prove the high value of *The Scream in Nature*.

Use the following passage for questions 28–30.

In its most basic form, geography is the study of space; more specifically, it studies the physical space of the earth and the ways in which it interacts with, shapes, and is shaped by its inhabitants. Geographers look at the world from a spatial perspective. This means that at the center of all geographic study is the question, *where?* For geographers, the *where* of any interaction, event, or development is a crucial element to understanding it.

This question of *where* can be asked in a variety of fields of study, so there are many subdisciplines of geography. These can be organized into four main categories: (1) regional studies, which examine the characteristics of a particular place; (2) topical studies, which look at a single physical or human feature that impacts the whole world; (3) physical studies, which focus on the physical features of Earth; and (4) human studies, which examine the relationship between human activity and the environment.

28

A researcher studying the relationship between farming and river systems would be engaged in which of the following geographical subdisciplines?

A. regional studies
B. topical studies
C. physical studies
D. human studies

29

Which of the following best describes the mode of the passage?

A. expository
B. narrative
C. persuasive
D. descriptive

30

Which of the following is a concise summary of the passage?

A. The most important question in geography is where an event or development took place.
B. Geography, which is the study of the physical space on Earth, can be broken down into four subdisciplines.
C. Regional studies is the study of a single region or area.
D. Geography can be broken down into four subdisciplines: regional studies, topical studies, physical studies, and human studies.

Use the following passage for question 31.

After World War 1, powerful political and social forces pushed for a return to normalcy in the United States. The result was disengagement from the larger world and increased focus on American economic growth and personal enjoyment. Caught in the middle of this was a cache of American writers, raised on the values of the prewar world and frustrated with what they viewed as the superficiality and materialism of postwar American culture. Many of them, like Ernest Hemingway and

F. Scott Fitzgerald, fled to Paris, where they became known as the "lost generation," creating a trove of literary works criticizing their home culture and delving into their own feelings of alienation.

31

In the third sentence, the word "cache" most nearly means

A. a group of the same type.

B a majority segment.

C. an organization.

D. a dispersed number.

Use the following passages for questions 32–40.

Passage One

In the field of veterinary medicine, the inquiry into whether animals experience pain the same way humans do is especially important in the context of pain management. Although many advancements have been made in research sciences and pain management is widely accepted as a necessary job of practitioners, a number of myths about animal pain still plague the field of veterinary medicine and prevent practitioners from making pain management a priority. According to veterinarian and writer Debbie Grant, three myths are especially <u>detrimental</u> to the cause.

The first is the myth that animals do not feel pain at all or that they feel it less intensely than humans; in fact, according to Grant, the biological mechanisms by which we experience pain are the very same mechanisms by which animals experience pain. Even the emotional reaction to a painful experience, like being afraid to return to the dentist after an unpleasant visit, is mirrored in animals.

The second myth that prevents the advancement of pain management practices is the myth that pain is a necessary part of an animal's recovery. While some veterinarians believe that pain may prevent a healing dog, for example, from playing too vigorously, Grant says this is simply not the case. In fact, restlessness and discomfort may even lead to unusually high levels of agitation and may consequently slow the recovery process even further.

Finally, contrary to the third myth, animals do not necessarily tolerate pain any better than humans do, though they may handle their pain differently. Grant emphasizes that veterinarians must be aware that a lack of obvious signs does not necessarily suggest that pain is not present: in fact, many animals are likely to conceal their pain out of an instinct to hide weaknesses that may make them easy targets for predators.

Passage Two

Unlike doctors, who typically have the benefit of discussing their patients' concerns, veterinarians cannot ask their patients whether and where they are experiencing discomfort. Additionally, veterinarians must be aware of the survival instinct of many animals to mask pain in response to the <u>foreign</u> environment of a veterinary office. For these reasons, diagnostic tools and strategies are instrumental in the effective practice of veterinary medicine.

Veterinarians have a unique challenge when it comes to diagnosing their patients. In 2014, researchers of veterinary medicine at the University of Perugia in Italy completed a review of the diagnostic tools and strategies available to today's practitioners and found a number of them to be effective. Presumptive diagnosis, the first of these strategies, involves making a prediction about the animal's pain based on the observable damage to the body or body part. In addition to presumptive diagnosis, veterinarians can use close observation to assess changes in the animal's behavior.

The most common tool for performing diagnosis is the clinical exam, which can include both a physical exam and laboratory testing. As part of this process, a veterinarian might make use of an objective pain scale, by which he or she could assess the animal's condition according to a number of criteria. This tool is especially useful throughout the course of treatment, as it provides the practitioner with a quantitative measure for evaluating the effectiveness of various treatment options.

32

As it is used in Passage One, the term "detrimental" most nearly means

A. mischievous.
B. damaging.
C. disturbing.
D. advantageous.

33

The author of Passage One most likely includes the example of the unpleasant dentist visit in order to

A. provide a relatable example of how pain can influence a person's emotions.
B. challenge the reader to overcome his or her natural, emotional response to painful experiences.
C. question a popular perception about the experience of going to the dentist.
D. highlight a similarity in the way humans and animals respond to pain.

34

As it is used in Passage Two, the term "foreign" most nearly means

A. unfamiliar.
B. inaccessible.
C. distant.
D. exotic.

35

The author of Passage One indicates that despite advancements in veterinary sciences, many veterinarians

- A. do not see the value in pain management practices for their patients.
- B. still employ outdated methods of pain management.
- C. still believe that pain management is a responsibility of the pet owner.
- D. still have misguided beliefs and practices related to pain management in animals.

36

The author of Passage Two indicates that veterinarians can improve their pain management practices by

- A. attempting to communicate with their patients about the pain they are experiencing.
- B. employing the best diagnostic practices in their field.
- C. encouraging pet owners to keep careful watch over their animals.
- D. inventing novel ways to assess and treat pain in animals.

37

The author of Passage Two indicates that objective pain measures are useful because

- A. they allow the veterinarian to compare an animal's pain level to the pain levels of other animals.
- B. they challenge the veterinarian to devise a treatment plan as quickly as possible.
- C. they discount the assumption that pain cannot be measured on an objective scale.
- D. they provide the veterinarian with a quantitative method for tracking pain levels over the course of an animal's treatment.

38

The author of Passage One would most likely respond to the discussion of presumptive diagnosis in Passage Two by

- A. asserting that substantial physical damage to an animal's form does not necessarily suggest the presence of pain.
- B. asserting that presumptive diagnosis is more effective for diagnosing humans and should not be used for diagnosing animals.
- C. asserting that similarities in methods of pain diagnosis for humans and animals are effective because of the biological similarities between them.
- D. asserting that veterinarians should not make use of presumptive diagnosis in evaluating and treating patients.

39

Which of the following best describes the relationship between the two passages?

A. The first passage makes the claim that pain management should be a priority for veterinarians, while the second passage rejects this claim.

B. The first passage emphasizes the veterinarian's responsibility to prioritize pain management in animals, while the second passage explores the tools by which veterinarians can execute this responsibility.

C. The first passage seeks to dispel myths about pain management in animals, while the second passage denies that they are myths.

D. The first passage sheds light on the shortcomings of veterinary sciences as they currently exist, while the second passage provides insight into how these shortcomings might be overcome.

40

Both authors indicate that veterinarians

A. must be aware that a lack of obvious symptoms does not necessarily suggest an absence of pain.

B. should make pain management for their patients a priority.

C. ought to be familiar with the misguided assumptions that exist in their field.

D. need to conduct a thorough examination before releasing an animal back to its owner.

Mathematics

Work the problem, and then choose the most correct answer.

1

The line of best fit is calculated for a data set that tracks the number of miles that passenger cars traveled annually in the US from 1960 to 2010. In the model, $x = 0$ represents the year 1960, and y is the number of miles traveled in billions. If the line of best fit is $y = 0.0293x + 0.563$, approximately how many additional miles were traveled for every 5 years that passed?

A. 0.0293 billion
B. 0.1465 billion
C. 0.5630 billion
D. 0.7100 billion

2

The graph below shows the number of months that Chicago, New York, and Houston had less than 3 inches of rain from 2009 to 2015.

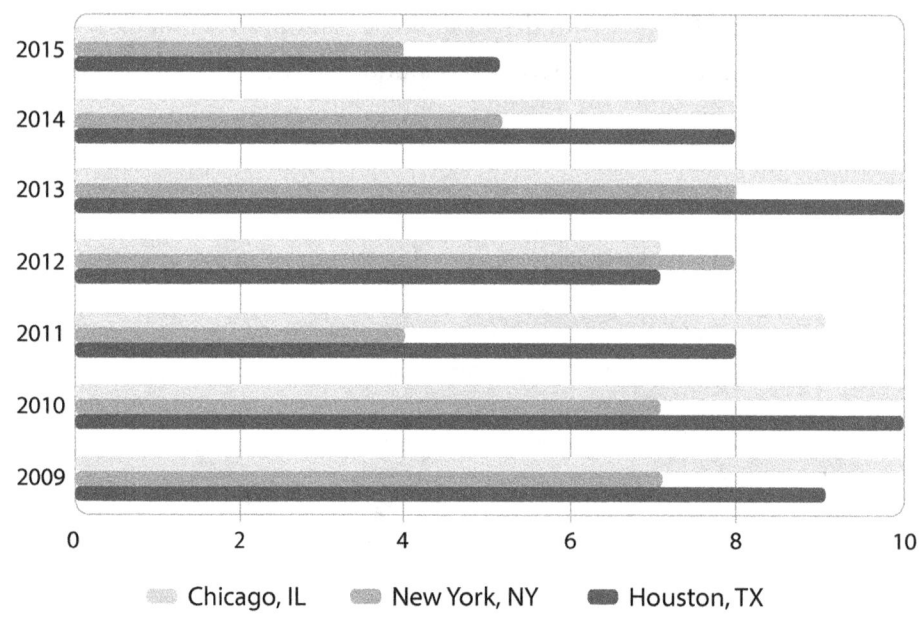

Number of Months with Less Than 3 Inches of Rain

From 2009 to 2015, what is the average number of months that Chicago had less than 3 inches of rain?

A. 6
B. 7
C. 8
D. 9

3

If a car uses 8 gallons of gas to travel 650 miles, how many miles can it travel using 12 gallons of gas?

A. 870 miles
B. 895 miles
C. 915 miles
D. 975 miles

4

Rectangular water tank A is 5 feet long, 10 feet wide, and 4 feet tall. Rectangular tank B is 5 feet long, 5 feet wide, and 4 feet tall. If the same amount of water is poured into both tanks and the height of the water in tank A is 1 foot, how high will the water be in tank B?

A. 1 foot
B. 2 feet
C. 3 feet
D. 4 feet

5

The figure below shows a rectangle with 4 square cutouts made to each corner. What is the area of the resulting shape?

A. 142 cm²
B. 200 cm²
C. 296 cm²
D. 320 cm²

6

The ratio of nurses to doctors in a hospital unit is 3:1. Which of the following could be the total number of nurses and doctors in the unit?

A. 28
B. 30
C. 31
D. 34

7

A group of 20 friends is planning a road trip. They have 3 cars that seat 4 people, 3 cars that seat 5 people, and 1 car that seats 6 people. What is the fewest number of cars they can take on the trip if each person needs his or her own seat?

A. 3 cars
B. 4 cars
C. 5 cars
D. 6 cars

8

Solve the following equation for y:
$3(2y + 1) + 3 = 4(y - 2)$

A. −7
B. −6
C. −1
D. 14

9

If a student answers 129 out of 150 questions correctly on a quiz, what percentage of questions did she answer incorrectly?

A. 10%
B. 12%
C. 14%
D. 15%

10

Solve the following equation for x:

6x − 7 = 5(2x + 1)

A. −3
B. −2
C. 4
D. 5

11

The formula for distance is d = v × t, where v is the object's velocity and t is the time. How long will it take a plane to fly 4000 miles from Chicago to London if the plane flies at a constant rate of 500 mph?

A. 3.5 hours
B. 8 hours
C. 20 hours
D. 45 hours

12

A semicircle is drawn next to the base of an isosceles triangle such that its diameter is perpendicular to the triangle's altitude. What is the area of the resulting figure shown below?

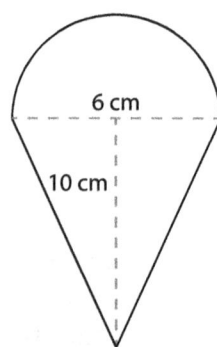

A. 30
B. 30 + 4.5π
C. 30 + 9π
D. 30 + 36π

13

Justin has a summer lawn care business and earns $40 for each lawn he mows. He also pays $35 per week in business expenses. Which of the following expressions represents Justin's profit after x weeks if he mows m number of lawns?

A. 40m − 35x
B. 40m + 35x
C. 35x(40 + m)
D. 35(40m + x)

14

An ice chest contains 24 sodas, some regular and some diet. The ratio of diet soda to regular soda is 1:3. How many regular sodas are there in the ice chest?

A. 4
B. 6
C. 18
D. 24

15

At the grocery store, apples cost $1.89 per pound and oranges cost $2.19 per pound. How much would it cost to purchase 2 pounds of apples and 1.5 pounds of oranges?

A. $6.62
B. $7.07
C. $7.14
D. $7.22

16

If 4x = 3, what is the value of 8x?

A. 0.75
B. 6
C. 12
D. 24

17

Which of the angles in the figure below are congruent?

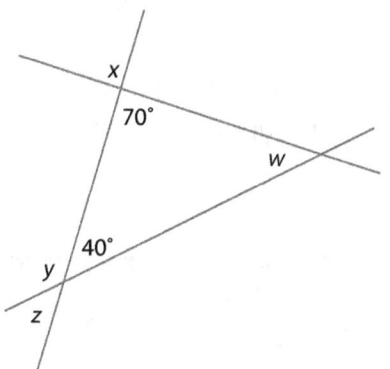

A. w and z
B. x and z
C. w and x
D. y and x

18

In the figure above, triangles ABF and CDE are equilateral. If the perimeter of the figure is 60 inches, what is the area of square BCEF in square inches?

A. 60
B. 100
C. 120
D. 144

19

Which of the following is the y-intercept of the line whose equation is $7y - 42x + 7 = 0$?

A. (6, 0)
B. (0, −1)
C. (−1, 0)
D. (0, 6)

20

Points W, X, Y, and Z lie on a circle with center A. If the diameter of the circle is 75, what is the sum of AW, AX, AY, and AZ?

A. 75
B. 100
C. 150
D. 300

21

Adam is painting the outside of a four-walled shed. The shed is 5 feet wide, 4 feet deep, and 7 feet high. How many square feet of paint will Adam need to paint the four sides of the shed?

A. 80
B. 126
C. 140
D. 252

22

If the volume of a cube is 343 cubic meters, what is the cube's surface area?

A. 49 m²
B. 84 m²
C. 196 m²
D. 294 m²

23

The mean of 13 numbers is 30. If the mean of 8 of these numbers is 42, what is the mean of the other 5 numbers?

A. 5.5
B. 10.8
C. 16.4
D. 21.2

24

Kendrick has $2386.52 in his checking account. If he pays $792.00 for rent, $84.63 for groceries, and $112.15 for his car insurance, how much money will he have left in his account?

A. $1397.74
B. $1482.37
C. $1509.89
D. $2189.22

25

In the fall, 425 students pass the math benchmark. In the spring, 680 students pass the same benchmark. What is the percentage increase in passing scores from fall to spring?

A. 37.5%
B. 55%
C. 60%
D. 62.5%

26

If one serving of milk contains 280 milligrams of calcium, how much calcium is in 1.5 servings?

A. 187 mg
B. 240 mg
C. 420 mg
D. 560 mg

27

Which of the following operations is equivalent to dividing by 100?

A. multiplying by $\frac{1}{100}$
B. adding −100
C. dividing by $\frac{1}{100}$
D. subtracting 100

28

If $5x + 2 = 2y$ and $y = 6$, what is the value of x?

A. 2
B. 3
C. 4
D. 5

29

What number is in the hundredths place when 21.563 is divided by 8?

A. 3
B. 5
C. 6
D. 9

30

Which of the following numbers is between $5\frac{1}{4}$ and $5\frac{1}{2}$?

A. $5\frac{5}{8}$
B. $5\frac{7}{20}$
C. $5\frac{3}{4}$
D. $5\frac{1}{10}$

31

What is the median of all the even integers greater than 10 and less than 25?

A. 14
B. 16
C. 18
D. 20

32

A fifth-grade teacher has her class check a rain gauge every day for five days. The students then draw their data on a graph as shown below.

What was the average daily rainfall over the five days?

A. 0.45 inches
B. 0.65 inches
C. 0.75 inches
D. 1.25 inches

33

Which of the following is equivalent to the term $5n$ for all values of n?

A. $5n^5 - n^4$
B. $3n + 2n$
C. n^5
D. $5 + n$

34

A 10 L container will hold how much more liquid than a 2 gallon container? (1 gal = 3.785 L)

A. 2.43 L
B. 6.22 L
C. 8.00 L
D. 9.47 L

35

A cyclist is moving down the sidewalk at 15 feet per second. What is his approximate speed in miles per hour?

A. 10.2 mph
B. 15.9 mph
C. 17.1 mph
D. 22 mph

36

Melissa is ordering fencing to enclose a square area of 5625 square feet. Which of the following is the number of feet of fencing she needs?

A. 75
B. 150
C. 300
D. 1405

37

If *ABCD* is a rectangle, which of the following statements must be true?

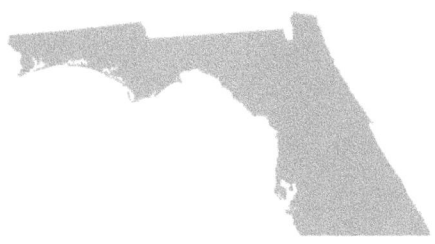

- A. $\angle AQD \cong \angle AQB$
- B. $\overline{AB} \cong \overline{AD}$
- C. $\triangle AQD \cong \triangle BQC$
- D. $m\angle AQB = 90°$

38

A circular swimming pool has a circumference of 50 feet. Which of the following is the diameter of the pool in feet?

- A. 25π
- B. $\frac{25}{\pi}$
- C. 50π
- D. $\frac{50}{\pi}$

39

Robbie has a bag of treats that contains 5 pieces of gum, 7 pieces of taffy, and 8 pieces of chocolate. If Robbie reaches into the bag and randomly pulls out a treat, what is the probability that Robbie will get a piece of taffy?

- A. $\frac{1}{7}$
- B. $\frac{7}{20}$
- C. $\frac{7}{13}$
- D. $\frac{13}{20}$

40

The pie graph below shows how a state's government plans to spend its annual budget of $3 billion. How much more money does the state plan to spend on infrastructure than education?

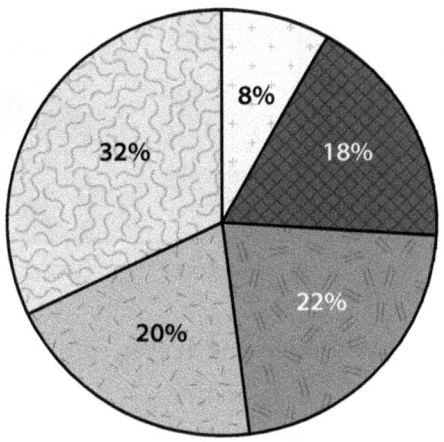

- Employees
- Education
- Healthcare
- Pension
- Infrastructure

- A. $60,000,000
- B. $120,000,000
- C. $300,000,000
- D. $540,000,000

41

The population of a town was 7250 in 2014 and 7375 in 2015. What was the percent increase from 2014 to 2015 to the nearest tenth of a percent?

- A. 1.5%
- B. 1.6%
- C. 1.7%
- D. 1.8%

42

Which graph shows the solution to y = 2x + 1?

A. B.

C.

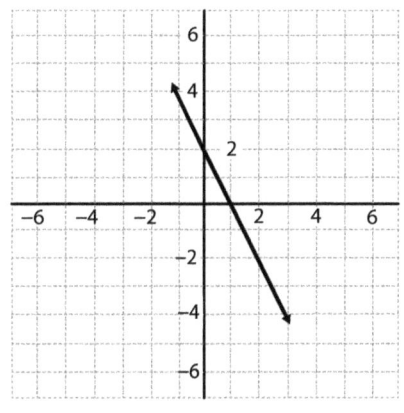

D.

43

Which of the following sets of coordinate points is NOT a function?

A. (3, 2); (4, 2); (5, 3); (8, 1)
B. (2, 2); (3, 2); (4, 2); (−1, 2)
C. (3, 4); (4, 2); (5, 3); (3, 1)
D. (−3, 2); (4, 2); (5, 3); (8, 1)

44

Solve the following inequality for x:

6x + 5 ≥ −15 + 8x

A. x ≤ −5
B. x ≤ 5
C. x ≤ 10
D. x ≤ 20

45

Which of the following symbols should be placed in the box to form a true statement?

$-\frac{3}{4}$ ☐ $-\frac{1}{2}$

A. >
B. <
C. ≥
D. ≤

Answer Key

The Essay

Violent storms are a huge risk to human life and property; they also have a strong impact on the economy, interfering with economic activity and sometimes damaging infrastructure. However, natural disasters are a fact of life on our planet, and it's impossible for economic development and growth to cease due to the possibility of a powerful storm. Still, rapid urban development is occurring in particularly storm-prone areas in Asia and even in North America, putting millions of people at risk. While the risks of a calamitous storm should never be underestimated, the solution is not to halt migration and slow economic growth, but to encourage investment in urban planning and public safety.

Centers of population in storm-prone areas in Indonesia, the Philippines, the United States East and Gulf Coasts, and elsewhere are indeed growing; natural resources and urban areas in these places are essential to local and national economies and even the global economy. During this time of change, especially in areas that are newly developing, opportunities for proper urban planning abound. Before growing urban areas get even larger, governments must take action to prevent the proliferation of slums, improve existing infrastructure to meet the needs of growing cities (or develop new infrastructure), and put policies into place for good urban management. Given the importance of these urban and industrial areas, especially for billion-dollar sectors like the oil and gas industry, there may even be opportunities for major companies to get involved in sponsoring urban development and safety in the economic zones and cities relevant to their interests around the world.

Furthermore, with economic growth also comes innovation and technology. Today, there are more opportunities than ever to develop products and procedures to ensure safety. From engineering to preparedness to emergency medical treatment, there are a plethora of approaches to storm readiness and flood control. Urban planning can take into account flooding and geographical impediments to emergency response time. There are more products on the market to help families survive for several days without help (for instance, water purifiers and other survival gear). Governments, civic organizations, and NGOs could be involved in emergency preparedness efforts and enlisted to distribute preparedness items during storm seasons, especially to those poor and working people who are the most likely to be affected and who would most likely be harmed. Using good technology and wise community coordination would ensure that vulnerable workers and their families are as safe as possible during storm season, so that they could benefit year-round from economic growth.

While storms and other natural disasters are and will remain a threat to human life, it's unrealistic to imagine that all economic activity will stop for the sake of safety. Thanks to economic growth and innovation, we can develop planning, technology, policy, and coordination to ensure the safety of communities as they drive the economic growth of those regions affected by major storms. That way, development can continue in as safe an environment as possible.

Writing

1)

A. **Correct.** "In addition" is the appropriate introductory phrase to signify the additive relationship between the two clauses.

2)

C. **Correct.** Here, all items in the list are nouns ("dearth," "lack," and "list"), followed by prepositions ("of") and objects of the prepositions ("wins," "time," and "clients").

3)

A. Incorrect. The modifying phrase "Invented in France in the early nineteenth century" incorrectly modifies "the modern form of the instrument" instead of "stethoscope." This is a dangling modifier.

B. Incorrect. The modifying phrase "Invented in France in the early nineteenth century" incorrectly modifies "several changes" instead of "stethoscope." This is a dangling modifier.

C. Incorrect. Joining these two independent clauses with a comma would make this sentence a comma splice.

D. **Correct.** "Invented," the past participle of "invent," appropriately introduces this modifying phrase that provides more information about the subject of the sentence ("stethoscope").

4)

B. **Correct.** *Which* is used correctly here to introduce an additional dependent clause describing the musical and correcting the comma splice.

5)

A. **Correct.** This information is unnecessary and detracts from the point of the passage.

6)

C. **Correct.** This is the clearest, most concise choice for communicating this idea.

7)

B. **Correct.** "In fact" can be used correctly in this instance to draw attention to interesting information that builds on the previous sentence.

8)

C. **Correct.** "Normalized" best expresses the idea that all "official" baseball bats are now the same shape, size, and weight. "Clarified" and "standardized" are not synonyms. "Reconciled" comes closer but does not make sense in context. "Ignored" and "standardized" are not synonyms.

9)

A. Incorrect. The verb phrase "is expecting to be" suggests that interstellar travel itself has expectations about the future.

B. Incorrect. The verb phrase "will be expected" is future tense, awkwardly suggesting that the mindset on interstellar travel does not yet exist. "Then" is used incorrectly to show comparison when it should refer to time.

C. **Correct.** The verb "is" is conjugated correctly in the present tense; "than" is used correctly to show comparison.

D. Incorrect. "Then" is used incorrectly to show comparison when it should refer to time.

10)

B. Correct. "Disrespectful" best expresses the idea that the students were behaving so rudely to their teacher that they deserved to be disciplined. "Confusing," "delightful," and "unlikely" do not make sense in this context.

11)

A. Correct. "Belligerent" means "hostile." The other answer choices—"sad," "worried," and "loud"—are not the best answers because a person may exhibit any of those characteristics without being hostile or combative.

12)

C. Correct. "Commonly" is an adverb describing "confused," which is an adjective describing "painters." The other choices are unnecessarily wordy.

13)

A. Correct. "Improving" best conveys the idea that Esperanto was intended to advance, or enhance, international communication. "Changing" and "advancing" are not synonyms. "Hastening" and "advancing" have related meanings, but they are not synonyms in this context, where "advance" means to improve. "Celebrating" and "advancing" are not synonyms.

14)

B. Correct. The three phrases share a structure; they are parallel adjectives.

15)

A) Correct. "Pilfering" means "stealing." If Karen had been "borrowing," "moving," or "returning" the newspaper, it is unlikely that Larry would have taken such drastic action.

16)

B. Correct. "Lucid" means "rational" or "clear." Answer choices A and D—"confused" and "incomprehensible"—are the opposite of "rational." Clyde may have been "emotional," but that does not explain why he was able to describe a person while in a stressful situation.

17)

D. Correct. The three phrases have a similar (parallel) structure (verb + direct object).

18)

B. Correct. "Callous" means "insensitive." A person may be "mean" or "annoyed" without being insensitive, so answer choices A and C are not the best choices. Answer choice D—"empathetic"—means the opposite of "callous" or "insensitive."

19)

C. Correct. *With* is the correct preposition for completing the prepositional idiom "combined with" and for communicating the intended meaning (that two things are combined *with* each other).

20)

C. Correct. The first clause ("Though the term...") is correctly joined to the second (independent) clause with a comma.

21)

C. Correct. "Apathetic" means "indifferent." If Omari was "satisfied" with his work, he would likely stay at his job. He is the opposite of "motivated." If he were "unsure" about his work, he might not be so quick to leave it.

22)

C. **Correct.** "Exacerbated" means to make something worse. "Hurt" is not relevant here; it is not possible to "hurt" a problem. "Reduced" means the opposite of "exacerbated." "Excited" lacks the negative connotation of "exacerbated" and does not make sense in context.

23)

B. **Correct.** "Conventional" best expresses the idea that the usual kind of comic book is told in many episodes about an established set of characters. "Normal" is subjective and unclear in meaning; it is not the best choice. "Traditional" and "expensive" are not synonyms; nor are "traditional" and "popular."

24)

D. **Correct.** This choice provides specific information, making it impactful and memorable.

25)

C. **Correct.** "Though" signifies an important contradiction between the two clauses in this sentence.

26)

A. Incorrect. This choice correctly forms two complete sentences.

B. Incorrect. This choice makes the second clause subordinate and appropriately joins the clauses with a comma.

C. Incorrect. This choice correctly joins two complete sentences with a semicolon.

D. **Correct.** This choice creates two complete sentences but joins them incorrectly with a comma, creating a comma splice.

27)

A. Incorrect. This choice provides unnecessary information that detracts from the main idea of the paragraph.

B. **Correct.** This choice is appropriately specific and provides a brief summary of the information mentioned in the paragraph.

C. Incorrect. This choice provides unnecessary information that is too specific to be an effective conclusion.

D. Incorrect. This choice provides unnecessary information that detracts from the main idea of the paragraph.

28)

C. **Correct.** Because the sentence states a general fact (how seat belts work), it should be written in the present tense.

29)

A. **Correct.** "Relatively" is an adverb that modifies "widely," an adverb that modifies the adjective "available."

30)

D. **Correct.** To "hinder" means to "impede." To "impede" is less severe than to "crush," which is to destroy something. Both "encourage" and "expedite" imply helping something to happen, which is the opposite meaning.

31)

D. **Correct.** To "foster" means to "strengthen" or "promote." Choice B, "create," is incorrect because it implies the relationships do not already exist. Choices A and C, "alleviate" and "discourage," imply the opposite of "promote."

32)

D. **Correct.** The two independent clauses are correctly joined with a coordinating conjunction ("and") and a comma.

33)

A. **Correct.** To "quantify" is to "measure" or determine the value of something. The other answer choices do not make sense in context; damage cannot really be "understood" as much as it can be measured, making choice A the best answer. Choices C and D, "extend" and "improve," do not make sense in this context. Damage is generally fixed rather than improved.

34)

A. **Correct.** "Frantic" means "panicked." "Calm" is the opposite of "frantic"; it is unlikely a father would be calm if he realized his child was missing. Answers C and D—"frustrated" and "upset"—are both incorrect because it is possible to be frustrated or upset without being frantic.

35)

C. **Correct.** The phrase "Before introducing self-driving vehicles" should modify "researchers." Only in choice C does this phrase directly modify that word. That modifying phrase is misplaced in choices A and B. In choice D, the modifying phrase "as early as the 1920s" is misplaced.

36)

A. **Correct.** "Abdicated" means to relinquish or give up to another. Answer choice C, "abandoned," is close in meaning but overly extreme; someone can relinquish a position or role without leaving irresponsibly. "Maintained" and "promoted" do not make sense in context.

37)

A. **Correct.** "Stealthily" means "furtively" or "secretly." "Fraudulently," choice B, is unrelated. Answers C and D, "brazenly" and "openly," are antonyms of "stealthily" and do not make sense in context.

38)

D. **Correct.** "Fields" best expresses the idea that members study many different categories of study, or disciplines. "Locations" and "regions" are not synonyms for "disciplines." "Discipline" and "punishment" are synonymous in some contexts, but the plural noun "punishments" does not make sense here. The sentence refers to fields of study, not punishment.

39)

B. **Correct.** This is the clearest and most concise way to convey the meaning of this sentence.

40)

C. **Correct.** "Persistent" means "unrelenting," which makes sense because Rhonda "could not get rid of" her "constant" cough. The other answer choices, "mild," "intermittent," and "bearable," do not make sense in this context.

ically **ANSWER KEY** 155

READING

1)

- A. Incorrect. While the author points out that jazz is often associated with New Orleans, he does not indicate that this is a problem or that people should change how they think about jazz.
- **B. Correct.** The author writes that "[j]azz music was played by and for a more expressive and freed populace than the United States had previously seen." In addition to "the emergence of the flapper," the 1920s saw "the explosion of African American art and culture now known as the Harlem Renaissance."
- C. Incorrect. Though this is mentioned in the passage, it is not the main idea.
- D. Incorrect. Though this is stated at the end of the passage, it is not the main idea.

2)

- **A. Correct.** The author writes that "[j]azz music was played by and for a more expressive and freed populace than the United States had previously seen." In addition to "the emergence of the flapper," the 1920s saw "the explosion of African American art and culture now known as the Harlem Renaissance."
- B. Incorrect. Though these artists are mentioned in the passage, the author does not indicate that they were the most important jazz musicians of the Harlem Renaissance, only that they were important.
- C. Incorrect. Though women's suffrage is mentioned in the passage, the author gives no indication that jazz music was the cause of this change.
- D. Incorrect. Though these artists are mentioned in the passage, the author does not indicate that they supported the movement for women's suffrage.

3)

- A. Incorrect. The author writes, "Jazz music also provided the soundtrack for the explosion of African American art and culture now known as the Harlem Renaissance." However, this is not the primary purpose of the passage.
- B. Incorrect. Though the author names many of the important jazz musicians who were playing during the 1920s, this is not the primary purpose of the passage.
- **C. Correct.** The author opens the passage saying, "In recent decades, jazz has been associated with New Orleans and festivals like Mardi Gras, but in the 1920s, jazz was a booming trend whose influence reached into many aspects of American culture." He then goes on to elaborate on what these movements were.
- D. Incorrect. The author discusses the effects of jazz music on arts and culture in the 1920s but does not go into the history of the art.

4)

- A. Incorrect. In the first paragraph, the author writes, "In fact, the years between World War I and the Great Depression were known as the Jazz Age, a term coined by F. Scott Fitzgerald in his famous novel *The Great Gatsby*."

B. **Correct.** At the end of the first paragraph, the author writes, "Ella Fitzgerald, for example, moved from Virginia to New York City to begin her much-lauded singing career, and jazz pioneer Louis Armstrong got his big break in Chicago."

C. Incorrect. At the beginning of the second paragraph, the author writes, "Women gained the right to vote and were openly seen drinking and dancing to jazz music. This period marked the emergence of the flapper, a woman determined to make a statement about her new role in society."

D. Incorrect. Toward the end of the second paragraph, the author writes, "Jazz music also provided the soundtrack for the explosion of African American art and culture now known as the Harlem Renaissance."

5)

A. Incorrect. The author states that the term *Jazz Age* was "coined by F. Scott Fitzgerald in his famous novel *The Great Gatsby*" but does not elaborate on Fitzgerald's relationship to the artists of the age.

B. Incorrect. The author does not discuss the current popularity of jazz, only that it is often associated with New Orleans.

C. **Correct.** The author writes that "[j]azz music was played by and for a more expressive and freed populace than the United States had previously seen." In addition to "the emergence of the flapper," the 1920s saw "the explosion of African American art and culture now known as the Harlem Renaissance."

D. Incorrect. The passage does not indicate that flappers and African American musicians worked together, only that they both used jazz music as a way to express themselves.

6)

A. Incorrect. The passage implies that "the physical and biological consequences of nuclear war" have impacts that reach much further than the military.

B. Incorrect. The second part of the second sentence suggests that the consequences of nuclear war—rather than the specific technology of nuclear weapons—are the focus of this student's paper.

C. Incorrect. The author mentions the decision by world powers to cease testing nuclear weapons in the atmosphere; however, this is only one detail and is likely not the focus of the essay as a whole.

D. **Correct.** The passage gives a short history of thermonuclear weapons and then introduces its main topic—the physical and biological consequences of nuclear war.

7)

D. **Correct.** The word "given" best describes the idea that the gifts have been handed out: "to the lion [Epimetheus] gave strength; to the bird, swiftness; to the fox, sagacity; and so on."

8)

A. **Correct.** The author writes, "But people who try to sell you this narrative are wrong. The Civil War was not a battle of cultural identities—it was a battle about slavery."

B. Incorrect. Though the author describes the cultural differences between the North and South in the first half of the passage, her primary purpose is revealed when she states, "But people who try to sell you this narrative are wrong."

C. Incorrect. The author makes no comment on the outcome of the Civil War.

D. Incorrect. The author asserts that, despite the popular identity narrative, the cause of the Civil War was actually very clear: "The Civil War was not a battle of cultural identities—it was a battle about slavery."

9)

B. Correct. The author states that the South's explanations for the war are "fanciful inventions" designed to cover up history, implying these explanations are imaginative or false.

10)

A. Incorrect. The author asserts that, despite the popular narrative, cultural differences were not the cause of the Civil War.

B. Correct. The author writes, "The Civil War was not a battle of cultural identities—it was a battle about slavery. All other explanations for the war are either a direct consequence of the South's desire for wealth at the expense of her fellow man or a fanciful invention to cover up this sad portion of our nation's history."

C. Incorrect. The author does not discuss the strengths of the North or provide any reason for why it won the war.

D. Incorrect. Though the author mentions these cultural beliefs, she does not suggest that these were the reasons the South was defeated.

11)

B. Correct. The author says that the house on Pine Street "had enough space inside but didn't have a big enough yard for [their] three dogs."

12)

A. Correct. The author argues that "every man, woman, and child should learn" to swim, and then explains to the reader why he or she should be able to swim.

13)

B. Correct. In February the service earned $1,100, and in April it earned $200. The difference between the two months is $900.

14)

A. Incorrect. The author's use of first person and exclamation marks signifies a more personal, less professional tone.

B. Correct. The author uses several markers of casual writing, including the first person, exclamation marks, and informal language.

C. Incorrect. The author writes that while recent months "have admittedly been a bit slow," she and her team are "hoping for a big summer once school gets out." While she recognizes that business has been slow, she does not seem concerned.

D. Incorrect. The author takes personal ownership over the business and expresses excitement about the busy Valentine's Day schedule and the upcoming summer.

15)

A. **Correct.** This detail is not stated in the passage.

16)

A. Incorrect. Thermometers that measure temperature in the ear and temporal artery are mentioned in the passage; however, they are a supporting detail for the author's primary purpose.

B. **Correct.** In the first paragraph, the author writes, "But what's the best way to get an accurate reading? The answer depends on the situation." She then goes on to describe various options and their applications.

C. Incorrect. Though this detail is mentioned, it is not the author's primary focus.

D. Incorrect. The author writes about how many people—not only nurses—use different types of thermometers in different situations.

17)

B. **Correct.** The author indicates that "[t]he most common way people measure body temperature is orally" but that "[t]here are many situations…when measuring temperature orally isn't an option." She then goes on to describe these situations in the second and third paragraphs.

18)

A. **Correct.** The final paragraph states that "agitated patients…won't be able to sit still long enough for an accurate reading." The reader can infer that an agitated patient is a patient who is visibly upset, annoyed, or uncomfortable.

B. Incorrect. While some agitated patients may move quickly, this is not necessarily the meaning of the word in context.

C. Incorrect. The term "violently ill" does not necessarily explain why a patient would have a difficult time sitting still.

D. Incorrect. The term "slightly dirty" does not explain why a patient would have a difficult time sitting still.

19)

A. **Correct.** The second paragraph of the passage states that "[u]sing the rectum also has the added benefit of providing a much more accurate reading than other locations can provide."

B. Incorrect. In the final paragraph, the author suggests that "certain people, like agitated patients or fussy babies," might have a difficult time sitting still but does not suggest that this is a problem for "many" people.

Answer Key

C. Incorrect. In the final paragraph, the author writes that "it's important to check the average temperature for each region, as it can vary by several degrees," but she does not cite this as a reason to use a rectal thermometer.

D. Incorrect. The author does not mention access to thermometers as a consideration.

20)

D. Correct. The author writes, "The army set high standards: all of the recruits had to be skilled on horseback."

21)

A. Correct. The author states that "[p]opcorn continued to rule the snack food kingdom until the rise in popularity of home televisions during the 1950s" when the industry saw a "decline in sales" as a result of the changing pastimes of the American people.

B. Incorrect. The author indicates that "the introduction of mobile popcorn machines" occurred "at the World's Columbian Exposition" after the Great Depression.

C. Incorrect. The author indicates that the primary reason people consumed popcorn during the Great Depression was that it was advertised as a "wholesome and economical food…a luxury that the downtrodden could afford." This implies that the cost, not the luxuriousness, of popcorn was its primary appeal.

D. Incorrect. The author indicates that "[t]he American love affair with popcorn began in 1912" and only after this did popcorn move "from the theater into fairs and parks."

22)

B. Correct. The author states, "For the Aztec Indians who called the caves home, popcorn (or *momochitl*) played an important role in society, both as a food staple and in ceremonies." This implies that the Aztec people popped popcorn both for special occasions ("in ceremonies") and for regular consumption ("as a food staple").

23)

A. Incorrect. The author mentions that popcorn was consumed "both as a food staple and in ceremonies" in Aztec culture but does not tie this to the popcorn industry in the United States.

B. Incorrect. The author indicates that growth in popularity of home televisions actually hurt the popcorn industry: "Popcorn continued to rule the snack food kingdom until the rise in popularity of home televisions during the 1950s" when the industry saw "a decline in sales."

C. Correct. The author writes, "The popcorn industry flourished during the Great Depression when it was advertised as a wholesome and economical food."

D. Incorrect. Though the nutritional value of popcorn is mentioned as a factor in its popularity during the Great Depression, the author does not indicate that this is the reason for its popularity in the United States.

24)

A. Correct. This statement summarizes the entire passage, including the brief history of popcorn in ancient cultures and the growth in the popularity of popcorn in America.

25)

A. Incorrect. Though the author does discuss the effect of the microwave on the popcorn industry ("it wasn't until microwave popcorn became commercially available in 1981 that at-home popcorn consumption began to grow exponentially"), this is not the primary purpose of the passage.

B. Incorrect. Though this may be true, it is not the primary purpose of the passage; the author traces the history of popcorn from ancient to modern times.

C. **Correct.** In the opening paragraph the author writes, "But popcorn isn't just for fun—it's also a multimillion-dollar-a-year industry with a long and fascinating history." The author then goes on to illustrate the history of popcorn from the ancient Aztecs, to early twentieth-century America, to the present day.

D. Incorrect. Though the author discusses the ancient Aztecs, the rest of the passage is focused on popcorn's history in American culture.

26)

A. Incorrect. The author writes, "In 1948, Herbert Dick and Earle Smith discovered old popcorn dating back 4,000 years in the New Mexico Bat Cave."

B. Incorrect. The author writes, "The American love affair with popcorn began in 1912, when popcorn was first sold in theaters."

C. **Correct.** The author writes, "However, it wasn't until microwave popcorn became commercially available in 1981 that at-home popcorn consumption began to grow exponentially. With the wide availability of microwaves in the United States, popcorn also began popping up in offices and hotel rooms."

D. Incorrect. The author writes, "However, the home still remains the most popular popcorn eating spot: today, 70 percent of the 16 billion quarts of popcorn consumed annually in the United States are eaten at home."

27)

A. Incorrect. The passage does not describe the actual artwork at all.

B. Incorrect. The author names the artist who made the painting but states nothing else about its origin.

C. Incorrect. While the author does state that there are four versions of the artwork, this is not the primary purpose of the passage.

D. **Correct.** The author writes, "*The Scream of Nature* by Edvard Munch is one of the world's best known and most desirable artworks."

28)

A. Incorrect. In regional studies, geographers "examine the characteristics of a particular place."

B. Incorrect. In topical studies, geographers "look at a single physical or human feature that impacts the world."

C. Incorrect. In physical studies, geographers "focus on the physical features of Earth."

D. **Correct.** The passage describes human studies as the study of "the relationship between human activity and the environment," which would include farmers interacting with river systems.

29)

- **A. Correct.** The passage explains what the study of geography involves and outlines its main subdisciplines.
- B. Incorrect. The passage does not include a story.
- C. Incorrect. The passage does not seek to change readers' opinions or behaviors.
- D. Incorrect. The passage provides information and facts but not descriptive details.

30)

- A. Incorrect. This is only one fact from the passage and does not represent an adequate summary of the passage as a whole.
- **B. Correct.** Only this choice summarizes the two main points of the passage: the definition of geography and the breakdown of its subdisciplines.
- C. Incorrect. This is only one detail from the passage and does not represent an adequate summary of the passage as a whole.
- D. Incorrect. This choice summarizes the second paragraph only and leaves out any summary of the first paragraph.

31)

- **A. Correct.** The author goes on to describe the shared perspectives of these writers.
- B. Incorrect. The author does not indicate the number of writers.
- C. Incorrect. The author provides no context that implies they were an organized group, simply that they shared certain traits.
- D. Incorrect. The author states that they gathered in one place—Paris.

32)

- A. Incorrect. This answer choice does not fit in the context of the sentence.
- **B. Correct.** The author writes that "a number of myths about animal pain still plague the field of veterinary medicine and prevent practitioners from making pain management a priority."
- C. Incorrect. The author does not imply that the myths are disturbing, only that they "prevent practitioners from making pain management a priority."
- D. Incorrect. The author indicates that the myths have a negative effect on the treatment of animals, not a positive one.

33)

- A. Incorrect. The author does not seek to make the experience of animals relatable, only to indicate that it is similar to the way humans experience pain and that it should be considered during the course of treatment.
- B. Incorrect. The author does not seek to change the behavior of the reader.
- C. Incorrect. The author does not challenge popular perceptions about the experience of going to the dentist; she only suggests that the experience is similar to that of animals in pain at the veterinarian's office.
- **D. Correct.** The author writes that "[e]ven the emotional reaction to a painful experience, like being afraid to return to the dentist after an unpleasant visit, is mirrored in animals."

34)

A. **Correct.** The author writes that animals mask pain in response to the "foreign environment of a veterinary office," implying that the office is unfamiliar to the animal.

35)

A. Incorrect. The author writes that "pain management is widely accepted as a necessary job of practitioners."

B. Incorrect. The author does not indicate that veterinarians employ outdated methods of pain management.

C. Incorrect. The author writes that "pain management is widely accepted as a necessary job of practitioners."

D. **Correct.** The author writes, "Although many advancements have been made in research sciences...a number of myths about animal pain still plague the field of veterinary medicine and prevent practitioners from making pain management a priority."

36)

A. Incorrect. The author does not suggest that veterinarians attempt to communicate with animals about their pain.

B. **Correct.** The author writes that "veterinarians must be aware of the survival instinct of many animals to mask pain in response to stressful experiences or foreign environments. For these reasons, diagnostic tools and strategies are instrumental in the effective practice of veterinary medicine."

C. Incorrect. The author suggests that veterinarians have a responsibility that extends beyond informing pet owners of the importance of close observation.

D. Incorrect. The author indicates that veterinarians should rely on existing "diagnostic tools and strategies available to today's practitioners" that have been found "to be effective." She does not indicate that veterinarians should invent their own methods for assessing and treating pain.

37)

D. **Correct.** The author writes that to diagnose pain in animals, "a veterinarian might make use of an objective pain scale, by which he or she could assess the animal's condition according to a number of criteria. This tool is especially useful throughout the course of treatment, as it provides the practitioner with a quantitative measure for evaluating the effectiveness of various treatment options."

38)

A. Incorrect. The author of Passage 1 gives no indication that physical damage and pain are unrelated.

B. Incorrect. The author of Passage 1 does not indicate that presumptive diagnosis is ineffective when used with animals.

C. **Correct.** The author of Passage 1 indicates that "according to Grant, the biological mechanisms by which we experience pain are the very same mechanisms by which animals experience pain." This indicates that the author believes that pain and the process of pain management are somewhat similar in animals and humans.

D. Incorrect. The author of Passage 1 does not indicate that presumptive diagnosis is ineffective when used with animals.

39)

A. Incorrect. The second passage does not reject the claim that pain management should be a priority of veterinarians.

B. Correct. The author of the first passage writes that "a number of myths about animal pain still plague the field of veterinary medicine and prevent practitioners from making pain management a priority." This implies that the author believes pain management should be a priority of veterinarians. The second author writes that "diagnostic tools and strategies are instrumental in the effective practice of veterinary medicine" and then goes on to describe some of these tools.

C. Incorrect. The author of the second passage does not contradict that the myths in the first passage are untrue.

D. Incorrect. The authors do not discuss shortcomings of veterinary medicine in broad terms; they only address the issue of pain management.

40)

A. Correct. The first author writes, "Grant emphasizes that veterinarians must be aware that a lack of obvious signs does not necessarily suggest that pain is not present: in fact, many animals, especially those that are prey animals in the wild, are likely to conceal their pain out of an instinct to hide weaknesses that may make them easy targets for predators." The second author agrees, saying that "veterinarians must be aware of the survival instinct of many animals to mask pain in response to stressful experiences or foreign environments."

B. Incorrect. While the first author indicates that pain management should be priority for veterinarians, the second author does not discuss the prioritization of pain management in relation to other responsibilities.

C. Incorrect. The first author seeks to dispel myths that exist in the world of veterinary medicine; the second author does not.

D. Incorrect. The second author indicates that thorough examinations must be conducted; the first author does not.

Mathematics

1)

B. The slope 0.0293 gives the increase in passenger car miles (in billions) for each year that passes. Multiply this value by 5 to find the increase that occurs over 5 years: $5(0.0293) =$ **0.1465 billion miles**.

2)

D. Use the graph to find the number of months Chicago had less than 3 inches of rain year, and then find the average.

Months with < 3 inches of rain in Chicago: {7, 8, 10, 7, 9, 10, 10}

$$\frac{7+8+10+7+9+10+10}{7} = 8.7 \approx 9$$

3)

D. Set up a proportion and solve.

$\frac{8}{650} = \frac{12}{x}$

$8x = (650)(12)$

$x =$ **975 miles**

4)

B. Calculate the volume of water in tank A.

$V = l \times w \times h$

$5 \times 10 \times 1 = 50$ ft^3

Find the height this volume would reach in tank B.

$V = l \times w \times h$

$50 = 5 \times 5 \times h$

$h =$ **2 ft**

5)

D. Find the area of the complete rectangle and subtract the area of the missing corners.

rectangle: $A = lw = (20 + 2 + 2) \times (10 + 2 + 2) = 336$ cm^2

corners: $A = 4(lw) = 4(2 \times 2) = 16$ cm^2

$336 - 16 =$ **320 cm²**

6)

A. If the ratio of nurses to doctors is 3:1, then the total number of nurses and doctors must be a multiple of 4 (because 3 + 1).

7)

B. Using the cars with the largest capacity first, add together the seats in the cars until there are 20.

$6 + 5 = 11$

$6 + 5 + 5 = 16$

$6 + 5 + 5 + 5 = 21$

The fewest number of cars that will seat 20 people is **4 cars**.

8)

A. Isolate the variable on one side of the equation.

$3(2y + 1) + 3 = 4(y - 2)$

$6y + 3 + 3 = 4y - 8$

$6y + 6 = 4y - 8$

$6y = 4y - 14$

$2y = -14$

$y =$ **−7**

9)

C. Subtract to find the number of questions the student answered incorrectly.

$150 - 129 = 21$

Use the formula for percentages.

percent $= \frac{\text{part}}{\text{whole}} = \frac{21}{150} = 0.14 =$ **14%**

10)

A. Isolate the variable on one side of the equation.

Answer Key

$6x - 7 = 5(2x + 1)$

$6x - 7 = 10x + 5$

$6x = 10x + 12$

$-4x = 12$

$x = \mathbf{-3}$

11)

B. Plug the given values into the equation and solve for t.

$d = v \times t$

$4000 = 500 \times t$

$t = \mathbf{8\ hours}$

12)

B. Add the area of the semicircle and the area of the triangle.

semicircle: $A = \frac{\pi r^2}{2} = \frac{\pi(3)^2}{2} = 4.5\pi$

triangle: $A = \frac{1}{2}bh = \frac{1}{2}(6)(10) = 30$

total area = $\mathbf{30 + 4.5\pi}$

13)

A. Justin's profit will be his income minus his expenses. He will earn $40 for each lawn, or $40m$. He pays $35 in expenses each week, or $35x$.

profit = $\mathbf{40m - 35x}$

14)

C. Solve the problem using a proportion. The ratio of diet to regular is 1:3, so the total number of sodas is a multiple of 4.

$\frac{3}{4} = \frac{x}{24}$

$4x = 3(24)$

$4x = 72$

$x = \mathbf{18}$

15)

B. Multiply the cost per pound by the number of pounds purchased to find the cost of each fruit.

apples: $2(1.89) = 3.78$

oranges: $1.5(2.19) = 3.285$

$3.78 + 3.285 = 7.065 = \mathbf{\$7.07}$

16)

B. Multiply each side by 2.

$4x = 3$

$2(4x) = 2(3)$

$8x = \mathbf{6}$

17)

C. Find the measure of each angle.

$m\angle w = 180 - (70 + 40) = 70°$

$m\angle x = 70°$

$m\angle y = 180 - 40 = 140°$

$m\angle z = 40°$

$\mathbf{\angle w \cong \angle x}$

18)

B. The sides in equilateral triangles are all the same length, and the sides of a square are all the same length. Because the triangles and the square share a side, all the lines in the figure are the same length. The perimeter can be used to find the length of one side:

60 inches ÷ 6 = 10 inches

Multiply two sides of the square to find its area:

10 in × 10 in = $\mathbf{100\ in^2}$

19)

B. The y-intercept (where the line crosses the y-axis) will have an x value of 0. This eliminates choices A, B, and D.

Plug $x = 0$ into the equation, and solve for y to find the y-intercept:

$7y - 42(0) + 7 = 0$

$7y = -7$

$y = -1$

The y-intercept is $\mathbf{(0, -1)}$.

20)

C. All the points lie on the circle, so each line segment is a radius. The sum of the 4 lines will be 4 times the radius.

$r = \frac{75}{2} = 37.5$

$4r = \mathbf{150}$

21)

B. Find the area of all sides of the shed. Two walls measure 5 feet by 7 feet; the other two walls measure 4 feet by 7 feet.

$A = 2l_1 w_1 + 2l_2 w_2$

$A = 2(5 \text{ ft})(7 \text{ ft}) + 2(4 \text{ ft})(7 \text{ ft})$

$A = 70 \text{ ft}^2 + 56 \text{ ft}^2 = \mathbf{126 \text{ ft}^2}$

22)

D. Use the volume to find the length of the cube's side.

$V = s^3$

$343 = s^3$

$s = 7 \text{ m}$

Find the area of each side.

$7(7) = 49 \text{ m}^2$

Multiply the area of each side by 6 to find the total surface area.

$49(6) = \mathbf{294 \text{ m}^2}$

23)

B. Find the sum of the 13 numbers whose mean is 30.

$13 \times 30 = 390$

Find the sum of the 8 numbers whose mean is 42.

$8 \times 42 = 336$

Find the sum and mean of the remaining 5 numbers.

$390 - 336 = 54$

$\frac{54}{5} = \mathbf{10.8}$

24)

A. Subtract the amount of the bills from the amount in the checking account.

$792.00 + 84.63 + 112.15 = 988.78$

$2386.52 - 988.78 = \mathbf{\$1397.74}$

25)

C. Use the formula for percent change.

percent change = $\frac{\text{amount of change}}{\text{original amount}}$

$= \frac{680 - 425}{425} = 0.6 = \mathbf{60\%}$

26)

C. Set up a proportion and solve.

$\frac{1}{280} = \frac{1.5}{x}$

$x = (280)(1.5)$

$x = \mathbf{420}$

27)

A. Dividing by 100 produces the same result as multiplying by $\frac{1}{100}$.

$n \div 100 = \frac{n}{100}$

$n \times \frac{1}{100} = \frac{n}{\mathbf{100}}$

28)

A. Plug in the given value for y and solve for x.

$5x + 2 = 2y$

$5x + 2 = 2(6)$

$5x + 2 = 12$

$5x + 2 - 2 = 12 - 2$

$5x = 10$

$\frac{5x}{5} = \frac{10}{5}$

$\mathbf{x = 2}$

29)

D. Divide and find the digit in the hundredths place.

$21.563 \div 8 = 2.6\underline{9}5375$

30)

B. Convert each fraction in the problem to a decimal.

$5\frac{1}{4} = 5.25$

$5\frac{1}{2} = 5.5$

ANSWER KEY 167

Convert each answer choice to a decimal, and find the value between 5.25 and 5.5.

Choice A: $5\frac{5}{8} = 5.625$

Choice B: $5\frac{7}{20} = 5.35$

Choice C: $5\frac{3}{4} = 5.75$

Choice D: $5\frac{1}{10} = 5.1$

$A = s^2$

$5{,}625 = s^2$

$\sqrt{5{,}625} = s$

$s = 75$ ft

Now multiply the side length by 4 to find the perimeter.

$P = 4s$

$P = 4(75$ ft.$) =$ **300 ft**

32)

C. List all the even integers greater than 10 and less than 25 in ascending order. The median is the value in the middle.

12, 14, 16, **18**, 20, 22, 24

37)

C. The diagonals of a rectangle create two sets of congruent triangles.

38)

D. The formula for the circumference of a circle is $C = 2\pi r$.

Because $d = 2r$, this formula can be rewritten:

$C = \pi d$

50 ft $= \pi d$

$d = \frac{50}{\pi}$

32)

B. To find the average, add the rainfall amounts and divide by 5.

$\frac{0.75 + 1.25 + 0 + 0.5 + 0.75}{5}$

$=$ **0.65 inches**

33)

B. Combine like terms.

$3n + 2n = 5n$

39)

B. Use the equation for probability.

$P($an event$)$

$= \frac{\text{number of favorable outcomes}}{\text{total number of possible outcomes}}$

$P = \frac{7}{5+7+8} = \frac{7}{20}$

34)

A. The answer choices are in liters, so convert gallons to liters.

2 gal $\times \frac{3.785 \text{ L}}{1 \text{ gal}} = 7.57$ L

Subtract to find the difference in liters.

10 L $- 7.57$ L $=$ **2.43 L**

40)

A. Find the amount the state will spend on infrastructure and education, and then find the difference.

infrastructure $= 0.2(3{,}000{,}000{,}000) = 600{,}000{,}000$

education $= 0.18(3{,}000{,}000{,}000) = 540{,}000{,}000$

$600{,}000{,}000 - 540{,}000{,}000 =$ **$60,000,000**

35)

A. Use dimensional analysis to convert feet to miles and seconds to hours.

$\frac{15 \text{ ft}}{\text{sec}} \times \frac{3600 \text{ sec}}{1 \text{ hr}} \times \frac{1 \text{ mi}}{5280 \text{ ft}}$

$\approx$ **10.2 mph**

36)

C. Use the area to find the length of one side of the square.

41)

C. Use the formula for percent change.

percent change $= \frac{\text{amount of change}}{\text{original amount}}$

$= \frac{7375 - 7250}{7250} = 0.017 = \mathbf{1.7\%}$

42)

A. The line $y = 2x + 1$ will have a slope of 2 and y-intercept of 1. The lines shown in graphs C and D have negative slopes. The line in graph B has a y-intercept of −2.

43)

C. For a set of points to be a function, there must be no more than one y-value for a single x-value. Choice C has two y-values for a single x-value: (3, 4) and (3, 1).

44)

C. Isolate the variable on the left side of the inequality. Reverse the direction of the inequality when dividing by a negative number.

$6x + 5 \geq -15 + 8x$

$-2x + 5 \geq -15$

$-2x \geq -20$

$\mathbf{x \leq 10}$

45)

B. $-\frac{3}{4}$ is less than $-\frac{1}{2}$.

To take your second FTCE General Knowledge practice test, follow the link:
www.cirrustestprep.com/ftce-general-knowledge-online-resources